For my family—my dad, my mom, and my brother.
We've been through so much together, and everything I am
carries pieces of you. Your strength, resilience, love, and
unity have shaped me in ways words can't fully capture.
This book is as much yours as it is mine. I love you.

A PURE JOURNEY

BECOMING THE TRUEST VERSION OF YOURSELF

DAMII

StoryBUILDERS PRESS

A Pure Journey: Becoming the Truest Version of Yourself

Published by StoryBuilders Press

eBook: 979-8-89833-024-8

Paperback: 979-8-89833-025-5

CONTENTS

INTRODUCTION

To whoever is reading this right now, the question is *why?*

What's your purpose for learning about a Pure Journey?

I think it's because you want to figure out if you're currently walking on one.

This read should unlock your mind and help you get a step closer to the answers you've been seeking.

A seeking heart is a heart that will always find.

To me, a seeking heart is someone who's open—open to learning and open to change.

You aren't stuck in your ways. You're leaning forward into the unknown, trusting that the answers you're looking for are out there, even if you don't get them all at once.

When you're on that quest for the *ultimate* answer, you end up finding other answers along the way—answers for wisdom, healing, direction, clarity, and growth.

You start picking up light even if you began in darkness. It's like what I pulled from Matthew in the Bible: "*Seek, and you will find.*"

The more you keep showing up for yourself, the more things start to shift. Darkness starts to lift. You begin to feel more alive. More true. More you. That's what the Pure Journey is all about.

I want you to read this text with your mind open. Take in the words and analyze them to see if they're part of your journey.

Not everyone knows how to Stay Pure. That's because most people don't fully know who they are yet.

When I say *Stay Pure*, I'm not talking about being perfect or the holiest in the room. I'm not talking about being a saint who never makes mistakes. *Stay Pure* isn't about living flawless; it's about living true.

The word *pure* means the truest form of something. To me, it's about being authentic—staying true to your values, your principles, and yourself. Not conforming to fit in. Not changing to be accepted. Not bending for the applause. It's staying you, even when life throws pressure your way.

And pure doesn't stop at identity. It's also how I describe the highest standard of anything. A pure hooper. Pure entertainment. Pure passion. In other words, this is as real as it gets, the truest form it can be.

That's the essence of *Stay Pure*, living as the most authentic version of yourself while striving to embody the best, most genuine form of whatever you do.

After all, nobody can do you better than you.

But discovering who you are takes time.

You become you through the fire. Through adversity. Through haters. Through silence. Through moments when you thought you were done. That's what forms identity. That's what sharpens purpose.

When you make it through, you can look back at the journey and see how it broke you, built you, and revealed you to yourself. That's what makes it Pure.

It didn't make you into someone else. It made you *you*.

The beauty of a Pure Journey is that all of ours look different, yet we go through the same key trials and tribulations that will lead us to our own unique destination. We all get tested. We all get pushed. If we *Stay Pure* while we keep walking, we all get refined.

I'm here to help you recognize your own Pure Journey.

To begin, ask yourself, *Am I being molded? Am I being revealed? Am I walking a Pure Journey?*

If you aren't yet, stay open to what you're about to discover as you turn the pages and tune in.

If you are, then keep walking with me and see what else you find.

Either way, this is your invitation to take your next step forward.

PART 1

YOU'LL THANK YOURSELF LATER

Before you can walk a Pure Journey, before you can even dream about becoming the version of yourself you know deep down you're meant to be, you gotta start with self-awareness.

I'm talking about the deep, sometimes painful, stare-at-yourself-in-the-mirror kind of self-awareness. It's the kind that forces you to say, *I'm not where I want to be, and it's nobody's fault but mine.*

Nothing changes until you can be real with yourself. If you're broke, you gotta be aware enough to say, *I need to make some money.* If you're slacking, you gotta say, *I've been off. I need to tighten up.* That's where growth starts. That's where the action kicks in.

But if you can't be honest, it means your ego's in the way. And ego? It will ruin your life in a soft, sneaky sort of way. It'll whisper *you're good* when you're not. It'll keep you fragile, scared of critique, and scared to break the illusion of your own perfection.

My brother always used to tell me in high school, *Kill your ego.* And I've had to do that over and over—even recently.

Even when I thought I was good, ego had me missing the fact that I needed to level up. You can have a good stretch, sure. But one win won't make you a champion.

Consistency does. Humility does. Self-awareness does.

If someone offers you criticism and your first instinct is to puff up, get defensive, and shut down, that's your ego.

If you can't say *I'm sorry*, if you can't admit when you're wrong, if you think you've outgrown being taught, that's your ego.

Trust me, ego will have you walking in circles, confusing noise for growth and comfort for progress. But the people who want to grow and change for the better, we keep our egos in check so we can stay in motion. That is where we have to start.

With truth. With awareness. With facing yourself and making the decision to grow. Welcome to Part 1. This is where the Pure Journey begins.

CHECK YOUR VALIDATION

Growing up, I was blessed. I had a mom who spoke life into me and my brother every single week.

She would sit us down, pull out the oil, and draw a cross on our foreheads. She'd pray for us. And then she'd speak.

You are handsome.

You are talented.

You are going to change the world.

My earliest memory of this was when I was five.

Imagine being in first grade, walking through the hallways, already believing *I can do anything* because someone told me over and over again that there were no limits on my life, that I was built for something great.

Growing up, I had a lot of kids around me who didn't really know themselves yet.

And I get it. We're young and learning life. But when you don't know who you are, it's easy to look at someone who does and take it the wrong way.

By the time I got to high school, some mistook my confidence for cockiness.

It was confusing because if you knew me back then, I was never in people's faces about anything.

I wasn't boasting. I wasn't saying I was better than anybody. I walked with my chest out and my head high because I knew what I could do.

For someone still trying to find their own footing, something about me rubbed them the wrong way.

They didn't know how to detect it.

They didn't know how to categorize it.

So they labeled it with a word they knew: *cocky*.

I remember being so bothered by it that I went home and asked my mom straight up, "Do you think I'm cocky?"

She calmly looked at me and said, "Nah. You just know yourself, and they don't."

That stuck with me my whole life. That's the real reason I moved the way I did back then. I wasn't trying to flex on anybody. I just had the confidence that had been built in me early. And a lot of kids didn't have that yet.

There's a big difference between confidence and cockiness. People blur the lines, but they're not the same at all.

Cockiness has arrogance in it. It's loud. It's boastful. You're focused on making yourself seem bigger by making others seem smaller. Instead of choosing to be better for you, you feel the need to be better than everyone else. There's no gratitude in it. Cockiness is rough and distasteful.

But confidence? Confidence is quiet. It contains an element of faith. It's trusting your work and believing in yourself without needing anyone else to be less than you.

That's what my mom gave me. A foundation. A voice I could trust even when the world around me got loud.

But I know some of y'all didn't grow up with that. Some of you never had a voice in your life that affirmed you, who saw your light before you saw it for yourself—who told you, *You matter, you're gifted, you're chosen.*

If that's you, hear me. You can still give that to yourself.

You can be the one who breaks the silence.

You can be the one who speaks life into yourself.

It's time to validate *yourself*—starting today.

Most people, especially in our generation, are looking to define themselves from the outside. Likes, comments, DMs, strangers online who don't even know them in any real way. That kind of identity doesn't hold any weight. It shifts with the algorithm. It fades when the world moves on.

Who you are has to come from *within,* from what's rooted deep down, from the voice you trust the most when everything else goes quiet. So what does that look like?

It looks like standing in front of a mirror, looking into your eyes, and speaking life. It might feel awkward at first. It might feel fake. But do it anyway because you're conditioning your mind, and the words you speak become the life you live—even if you don't believe it yet.

Start simple: *Today is going to be a great day,* or, *I'm going to have a great day.*

Say it even if it feels shaky. Say it if the evidence isn't there yet because the words you say to yourself carry power. If you keep speaking life, you'll actually start to live. I've seen it in my own story. There were things I said out loud before I ever saw them in real life. But over time, those words became real.

It's the same if you choose the other way. If all you speak is death, defeat, and doubt, you'll start to live like it. That's why you have to be intentional about what you're pouring into yourself.

Don't wait on someone else to tell you who you are. Don't wait on a crowd or a comment section.

Affirm yourself. Bless yourself. Anoint yourself. The more you build yourself up, the easier it is to get even more real with yourself.

And watch what happens when you finally believe it.

CHECK YOUR DISCIPLINE

My dad was a different kind of teacher.

He didn't say much, but the way he moved taught me everything. I watched him walk through life with one mission: *provide for my family, no matter what.*

He didn't care if people misunderstood him. He wasn't interested in looking soft or sweet for the outside world. He was okay with being misjudged if it meant doing what was right for the ones he loved. That kind of strength isn't loud. It isn't flashy. But it's real.

When it came to raising my brother and me, my dad sacrificed being liked for being honest. He chose discipline over comfort. He chose structure over our approval. And now, as a grown man, I get it.

Back then, I thought he was too hard. Too serious. Too cutthroat. *Why is he always on us? Why can't he just relax?*

But now, I see the fruit of what he planted. I see the man I've become. And I know I wouldn't be this version of me without the father who wasn't afraid to be misunderstood.

He was training us. Sharpening us. Turning boys into men.

Now we laugh more. There's space for play. But even in the way he's mellowed out, you can tell he already did the hard part. The seeds were planted.

He didn't need validation from me or anyone else back then because he knew his *why.* He knew his intention.

And everything he did—every rule, every curfew, every hard conversation—came from love, from a man who showed *I'll be the villain if I have to as long as it makes you strong.* And for that, I love him even more.

Discipline isn't about denying yourself; it's about setting yourself up for a better tomorrow. It's making the hard choices now, trusting they'll pay off when the time is right.

Discipline is the ultimate form of self-love. So how much do you truly love yourself?

When the urge to quit hits, remind yourself that the grind you put in today will result in a gift you'll be unwrapping tomorrow.

CHECK YOUR SURROUNDINGS

Ask yourself this: *Are the people around me pulling me up or dragging me down? Are they filling me with light or feeding the darkness?*

If you're constantly around negativity, whether it's toxic friends, music that drains you, a post on social media that discourages you, or a relationship that breaks your spirit, you'll start to absorb that energy. You'll start thinking, *Maybe I'm not worth it. Maybe I am what they say I am.*

But you're not. You were just soaking in the wrong sound.

To walk a Pure Journey, you have to filter your spirit. Fill it with light. With truth. With words that build you instead of words that break you. And sometimes, that voice has to be your own because once you realize that your opinion of yourself is the most important voice in the room, you'll feel the shift. You'll feel the power of hearing yourself say, *I got this.*

You'll stop waiting for the world to tell you who you are because you already know.

And while you're checking the voices around you, make sure you're checking the voice *inside you* too.

Sometimes it's not your circle that's breaking you down; it's your mindset.

There's a thin line between motivation and comparison, and where you choose to land can change everything.

Motivation is when you see someone doing their thing and it lights a fire in you. It's like, *I see you winning, and it makes me want to tighten up my own walk.*

You admire their discipline. You clap for them with your whole heart. And then you get up and go do your thing with that same energy.

That's genuine. That's Pure.

But comparison? They call it the thief of joy for a reason. It's envy in disguise.

It's when you see someone's success online and start asking, *Why not me?*

That's not love. That's emptiness. A dead end. It doesn't ever build you. It breaks you slowly and silently.

That's why I say, focus on you until the focus is on you.

The same post will hit differently depending on how solid you are with yourself.

If your spirit is full, you'll see it and say, *Man, I'm proud of them, and I'm next.*

But if your heart's empty, you scroll past—bitter—thinking, *They got it. I'll never have it. They don't deserve it.*

Which one are you?

That's why you have to focus on cooking in your own kitchen. Perfect your recipe. Serve your own table because when you focus on yourself, you stop measuring your walk by someone else's path. You stop questioning your timing. You stop letting envy steal your joy.

A Pure Journey isn't about being first. It's about remaining true when the spotlight isn't on you fully and freely. So clap loud for others. Let their wins feed your drive, not your doubt.

There's greatness in your kitchen if you keep cooking.

CHECK YOUR CONSISTENCY

On this journey, you will find yourself trying a lot of different things and figuring out what works for you. It's all part of it, and it's an unavoidable line in the script. However, you won't start finding any answers until you seek them every day.

Consistency, consistency, consistency. Man, that's the name of the game, bro. Don't get much simpler than that. If you keep going every single day and don't stop, your competition will fall off, bro. These folks ain't cut like you, bro. They ain't ready for prime time. They ain't trying to really get it right. They take days off, this day off, that day off. "They lazy. I'm tired." No. Grind every day, one foot in front of the other, bro. And I promise you, you gonna be lapping these folks, bro. Give it a year and watch what happens.

Every day means you're consistent, and a key component when it comes to becoming successful and mastering any craft is consistency.

Consistency is a combination of willpower, diligence, and perseverance. It can singlehandedly change your situation based just on the strength of the action. The problem with being consistent is that most people can't consistently be consistent; they eventually fall off. The ones who keep going are the relentless dreamchasers of this world, and they have a grit in them that is not teachable.

In order to figure out what you are made of, you *must* be on a consistent pursuit in life.

To bring this trait out of yourself, you need to establish your purpose for doing the task at hand.

CHECK YOUR WHY

Let's be honest. It's hard to commit to something every day when you don't know why you're doing it. Maybe you want to be successful, financially independent, or respected. And with that, you need to make it personal.

When I started making achieving a goal personal, my own validation toward myself heightened, which is very important. I started to compete with the results I gained the day prior, trying to beat what I just did. Getting up day in and day out and conquering the day will have you set a standard for yourself that you know you need to meet.

With that mindset, it should provoke the next element to achieve consistency, which is legacy.

When you are desiring to be consistent, think about the legacy you want to leave behind. You're playing the long game, and you want each step you're taking to be one that is a step toward a legacy. Being consistent is a draining and daunting trait, so in times when you can't find the desire to keep going, revisit your purpose and remind yourself why you started. You always have to remember that.

I ain't gonna lie
to you bro. You kinda
frustrate me, bro because there's
no secret formula for
success and you
making it
hard. It's very
simple. You
stay disciplined
and you grind.
Every day. Repeat,
repeat, repeat. Is that
something you're ready
for, or are you soft? It's gotta
be something you answer yourself,
my boy.

If you want to achieve something great, you have to be focused. No shortcuts. No days off. You can't just want it when you feel like it or when it's convenient—you've got to be all in, even when you're tired, even when you're not motivated.

That's where discipline comes into play. It's what separates the ones who achieve from the ones who give up.

I developed a super-high focus when I was playing basketball in high school. When I was growing up, baseball was my main sport, but when I got into ninth grade, the baseball program was way too expensive. My father told me to pick a different sport or focus on academics. I chose basketball because my brother played it, and it was the next sport I had the most interest in.

Naturally, I was more athletic than a lot of kids and could play basketball due to just playing outside recreationally. However, my goal wasn't to make a basketball team just to say I was on it. I genuinely wanted to be the best, and I had to develop an intense focus because ultimately I was playing catch-up to the players who had been playing their whole lives.

I knew I was working a lot harder than my peers, and the main thing that separated me from them was working when I didn't feel like it. The simple fact that I worked when most people chilled was how I caught up to my peers in just one year of seriously playing basketball. I couldn't afford to train only when I was motivated.

Everyone always speaks about their motivation going on and off. Welcome to reality. We aren't robots. Discipline makes you consistent, consistency brings results, and results will motivate you. But the real question is this: *How long can you go without seeing results?*

If you're not ready for the level of consistency where you're going months or maybe years without seeing results, then you need to be real with yourself about whether you're serious about your goals. This journey isn't for the weak. It's for those who are tired of sitting around waiting for an opportunity to come and are ready to snatch the life they want to live because they know no one's going to hand them success.

CHECK YOUR TIMING

If you're waiting for the perfect time, you're fooling yourself.

The perfect opportunity is an illusion that keeps people in a never-ending revolving door. Right now is the only time you have because tomorrow isn't promised. You need to come to the realization that when you wait, you're wasting an opportunity that others are dying to have.

The truth is, if you wait, you don't deserve success. Success doesn't come to people who just want it; it comes to people who take it.

At the end of the day, you gotta go get up and go get it. I don't know what you're waiting on, the perfect opportunity, the perfect time. Ain't no such thing as the perfect time. Get that out of your head. The time is right now, and you're blowing it.

You know how many people would kill to have your opportunity, and you're just letting it slip away? Why are you acting like you deserve this? You don't deserve this. People want what you got. You're playing with your food. You keep playing with your food, someone's gonna come up and eat off your plate. That's really gonna hurt.

You'll wake up one day, though. For better or for worse.

That reminds me of the cycle we see at the end of every year. I notice that when it gets to about October or November, people start saying how they will start their plans on January 1. Honestly, that doesn't make any logical sense. They think there is some kind of magic potion on January 1 that will provoke them to start, but truthfully, if you aren't willing to start now, you won't start later.

CHECK YOUR EXCUSES

I take procrastination personally, and I make it a mission to limit it as much as I can. My thought process with procrastination is that the more I push my goals back, the less time my family and I get to enjoy the fruits of my labor.

The reality of procrastination is that each day you play with your future, you are pushing back what's months or even years for you. Or even worse, someone who's more focused and hungrier than you is going to take what was supposed to be yours.

You're going to wake up one day and really see what you did, either seeing it with satisfaction for going all in or with regret for letting it slip away.

Imagine you leave your food outside all day. It gets cold, and insects and birds eat it up. Now apply that to your dreams.

You're letting them go to waste or giving other people an opportunity to take what's yours.

You have to protect your dreams. Treat them like they're your child, and understand that the dreams are God-given, just for you. Think about it. If God gave you a gift, why would you choose to set it aside without opening it and using it? Ultimately, your procrastination is a sign of disrespect to God and an underlying sign of laziness.

Hey bruh, I ain't
  think I have to
  be the one to tell
you, but you can't be lazy
  and make it. The ones who grind,
    get it. Period. You can't be
    sitting here every
    day being piss
poor expecting
to be successful.
    That's not
    how it works.
    Every single day,
    it's clockwork. Grind.
      And what you do is not
gonna cut it. So don't be sitting
    here surprised when you living
    an average life because you doing
      average things. Simple as that.

If you're serious about becoming successful, laziness can't be part of the equation. I know you've probably heard it thousands of times before, but it needs to hit you in the core of your soul—work ethic is a non-negotiable in the contract of becoming successful.

You can't expect to climb up in life while sitting around, doing the bare minimum, and complaining about your circumstances. Everyone has issues.

The statement "life is unfair" is actually one of the biggest lies and coping mechanisms known to mankind. I say this because life is actually very fair since it is unfair to everyone. We just have to look at our unfair life and figure out how to maneuver through it, just like everyone else.

I suggest you rewire your mindset and start taking every day for what it actually is—an opportunity. Thinking with the perspective that millions of people died today yet you were one of the ones who made it is a powerful revelation. Seeing the next day means you were gifted another opportunity to get this right.

It's easy to get caught up in excuses or distractions, but those who succeed make a habit of showing up and putting in the work, even when they don't feel like it. This has to be a lifestyle.

If you're finding yourself stuck or not where you want to be, ask yourself this: *Am I really giving everything I've got to this?* Sometimes what we think is hard work is really just going through the motions. If you're being honest, you'll recognize that half-assed efforts lead to half-assed results.

CHECK YOUR HABITS

If you want to change your life, start by changing your daily habits. Build a routine that centers on discipline and focus. Stop chasing quick fixes, and put in the real work that leads to lasting success.

Find a system that pushes you to improve, even when it feels uncomfortable. Success doesn't come from comfort; it comes from grit, resilience, and consistency. And when you get into that mindset, you'll realize there's no room for laziness.

I'm saying this to wake you up to what's possible when you commit fully. If you're tired of living an average life, stop putting in average effort. Live every day with intention and purpose, and watch how your life transforms. You'll realize that by living this way, you're giving yourself power to control what you can control. Understanding the power you have is a big turning point on your journey.

Six months.
You know exactly what
you need to do this year. Get you
a better diet, go to sleep
early, wake up
early, work
out, read a
book. Get off
your phone
and focus. I
guarantee if you
give me six months
of that, you'll change
your life.

I feel like every person who wants to escape mediocrity and take control of their life needs to dedicate six serious months to develop good habits.

Why six months?

Do you understand how much time that is and how much can change in that time period?

1. It takes on average sixty days to form a new habit or get rid of a bad one.

2. To see measurable progress like physical transformation, skill-building, or mental shifts, six months is long enough to see those.

3. Overall, six months of focused effort can lead to a lifestyle change, not just a temporary boost.

If you lock in for six months, everything you gain during that period could legitimately save you from encounters or challenges you may face ten or fifteen years from now. It's a butterfly effect.

We often get caught up in excuses, distractions, and wrong habits, thinking there's always more time. But like I said before, time is the most valuable thing we have, and every day you waste is a day you can't get back.

The biggest hurdle on your journey is your own discipline. The hardest part isn't figuring out what to do; it's just doing it. The phone, the endless scrolling, the excuses—they're all pulling you away from your potential. But are you actually going to change that?

Six months of focus could be the time you need to set yourself up for the remainder of your life. Stop making excuses, and stop waiting for the perfect moment. It'll never come. If you give yourself six months of a relentless focus, I promise you'll look back and notice how far you've come.

It's on you. You can transform your life or stay the same. But don't expect results without putting in work. After developing into the person you are supposed to be, you'll notice you start moving like a winner every single day—and that's so important.

Winning is something many feel they are doing, but they simply aren't.

Hey, Dawg.
Look, you
wanna know how
you gon win? You treat
every day like a Monday and
every month like a January.
You gotta wake up
every day and
put 110 percent
to your craft
because there's
someone out
there that's getting
it more than you. So
don't be acting shocked
when they up and you down.
The person who grinds the hardest
always gets it.

Hard work beats talent every time.
Remember that.

One of the biggest formulas to winning is to treat every day with the urgency and intensity that people usually save for Mondays and every New Year. Why? Because that's when most people are usually the most motivated—setting goals and going after what they want.

But individuals who do that are just living with a losing mentality. No one who actually wants the most out of this life will put in maximum effort only on a certain day or time of the year.

Is that person you? Don't lie to yourself because you won't break out of this mentality without being honest with yourself.

Ask yourself who you are right now and who you want to become. You should want to become a winner.

Attacking each day with intensity and focus is hard to maintain because we're not robots. I'm not telling you to burn yourself out; however, it's all about the mentality you have toward each day. It's about your desire and passion to win.

This feeling in your soul will move you and propel you to dominate most of your days. Some days you will have to take your Ls and learn, but if you're doing more than your competition, how could you *not* win?

CHECK YOUR PATIENCE

Please understand this reality: *Your dream isn't only yours.*

Plenty of people are out there hungry, just like you. A winning mentality is so important because on this journey, when you're competing with millions of others who are chasing the same thing you are, the person who is taking the minor detail precautions comes out on top.

But I want to tell you this: Don't race them. Go at your own pace, and stay patient.

I remember running races when I was on the track team. Someone would have a lead on me early, but I wouldn't panic. I wouldn't get too caught up in the fact that they were ahead because I knew there was a long way to go.

Maybe they started off fast. Cool. But when that last stretch came, that's when I ramped it up and caught them.

And that's real life too.

Someone might jump out hot right after college. They might get the job first. They might hit some early success.

But ten years later?

You're the one who's thriving. You're the one who's still rising while they're still sitting in the same place. You ran your race.

Everybody's caught up in *right now*. Who's hot. Who's making moves now. But if you're really about journey, you're building for longevity, not just a moment.

So don't rush. Don't compare. Trust your pace. Trust your journey.

The goal is to be the one who's still standing tall tomorrow.

See, look, one
thing I want you
to promise me is
that no matter how long
it takes, keep going. No matter
how much it hurts, keep going. So you
were placed on this earth for a
reason.

You weren't meant
to be average.
You were meant
to excel. You
gotta understand
that this grind is
meant to make you
who you're supposed to
be. A dawg.

A little grind ain't never hurt
nobody. Stop being soft. Let's
embrace it. If you go through that fire,
you're gonna come out real cold. That's
what we want.

I know you want it bad, and I know you wish you could fast-forward to the life you pray for every day.

I would be lying to you if I said patience is easy. Patience is so intricate because it involves balancing immediate desires with long-term goals, which often counter our human nature. Our natural human tendency is to desire instant rewards and gratification.

Think about the world we live in. Everything is fast. We can warm our food in sixty seconds, have instant communication, and demand next-day shipping. As a society, we have been spoiled by the luxury of *instant*.

Patience requires a type of discipline that goes against our instincts, which makes it very challenging to develop. Patience requires you to trust that your efforts will pay off down the line, which can make you uncertain or uncomfortable. But you have to trust yourself because you're all you got. No one is going to do the work for you and come and save you. Believe in your abilities and trust that you're building a foundation that won't crumble when it's your time to show out.

No matter how tough or long the journey is, the only way you'll reach your full potential is by pushing forward with that blind faith. On the other side of patience and belief is the life that you've been praying for. You will have nights where you question if it's for you, nights where you cry or think about giving up.

But what most people don't understand is that the hurt you feel is right before your breakthrough. Don't let temporary feelings and your lack of patience block you from receiving your blessing.

You were put on this earth for a purpose, and that purpose isn't to be a failure. You are meant to do big things in this world, and the adversity you go through isn't there to break you; it's there to make you.

Embrace the struggle. Don't run from it. *You'll thank yourself later.*

PART 2

HATE GON' MAKE YOU GREAT

Hate is one of the most inevitable and damaging experiences you'll ever face, but only if you let it. It's easy to let criticism, negativity, or jealousy eat away at you, but there's another way to channel that energy. Every person who doubted you, talked down to you, or tried to bring you down can be the spark you need to rise. Hate doesn't just push you; it can propel you. Let it be the fuel for your fire, not the weight holding you down. When others try to dim your light, let their shadows remind you of how bright you truly are.

The first step on your Pure Journey is checking on the internal factors that are affecting your ability to Stay Pure. Next, you gotta recognize what hate is.

Hate is when somebody sees something in you—a light, a gift, or even self-confidence—and instead of being inspired by it, they feel threatened.

Hate isn't just loud boos or trash talk. Most of the time, it's little side comments, fake jokes, or just weird energy.

It's envy.

It's jealousy.

It's fear.

It's a parasite that feeds on your light because it doesn't know how to shine on its own.

Sometimes hate comes dressed up as advice or concern. Sometimes it comes from people you thought were your friends. It's the people closest to you who have the hardest time clapping when you win. That's life.

While you're working on yourself and stacking wins every day, you will encounter people who can't handle it. That's inevitable. People who aren't doing anything in their lives look at you and see what they aren't.

Staying Pure means that even when naysayers are trying to distract you, you stay rooted to your vision.

A lot of times we care about what people think so much that we start believing that what they're saying about us is true, which can end our dreams for good.

Think about whether you want to let someone who is miserable and insecure with themselves deter you from goals and aspirations that could change your whole family's bloodline.

That sounds crazy, doesn't it?

You have to protect your energy, be laser-focused, and channel the negativity as fuel.

Once you know what hate really is, you stop taking it personally.

My brother told me about this early when I was in sixth grade. He said, "You're gonna have a lot of haters, and a lot of people are not your friends." I actually saved that screenshot. It planted a seed early.

That stuck with me.

Before I even experienced my first real hater, I had already decided that *I just don't care about what people have to say.*

So when the hate came, I was already prepared for it.

I think you just
gotta wake up
one day and just say,
so what? Like, who cares if
they don't believe in me? I believe
in myself. You've put
too much work
into not have
this amount
of confidence,
and if you don't
believe in me, it
doesn't change my
success story. I'm still
gonna win. But I guess one
thing I gotta say is, let me know
when that hate starts making
you money.

EMBRACE THE HATE

Think of everything negative as a way to increase the intensity even more. Every hater is a reminder that you're doing something significant. If you weren't, they wouldn't bother you. No one tries to tear down something that isn't built.

Remember that.

In anything competitive, you do need a little bit of an edge.

You need that little bit of healthy ego to want to win—to want to get better.

Otherwise, you'll just stay comfortable.

But it can't get to the point where it's toxic.

Where you can't take criticism.

Where you think you're untouchable.

For me, it usually came out in sports.

If I told you I was going to do something and then did it, I might say, "I told you!"

Not to put anyone down or to say "you suck."

It's just my way of wanting to stand by my own belief in myself.

Walking around every day like you're better than everybody? Nah, that was never me. I made sure of that.

Sometimes people are gonna hate on you along your journey. They're gonna throw labels and dirt on you that they don't even understand. But you can't let it kill your spirit or take you away from your path.

I remember my junior year of high school when I was getting "overrated" chants during basketball practice. I was so confused because I just didn't understand at that time why people willingly hated on you for no reason at all.

I realized later that it was their own insecurities projecting onto me.

Those people saw me as such a threat that they felt they needed to chant like fans to affect my game. Times like those really molded my mindset into what it is now.

I started to understand that people who do this are truly the audience in your come-up story.

Understand that they'll always have something to say— positive or negative—but how you respond and what you choose to internalize is up to you.

At sixteen or seventeen, I met my first real hater—and it wasn't a stranger. It was someone who was supposed to be a mentor. My high school basketball coach, the person who should have built my confidence, was rooting against me. Behind closed doors he acted supportive, but in public he tore me down and disguised it as "coaching." He crossed lines no coach should cross, attacking where my family came from, dismissing my work, and even telling me to transfer schools. It wasn't tough love; it was hate. And when a coach sets that tone, the players follow. It trickled down. My teammates joined in, discrediting me and piling on. That coach wanted to embarrass me into quitting, but quitting was never an option. That only made him push harder to break me. As a kid, you don't forget that kind of treatment. But looking back, I'm grateful. It taught me early that sometimes even the people on your own team will go against you.

Honestly, that's when it hit me. Even when you're locked in, doing exactly what you're supposed to be doing, you're not protected from hate. Nobody is. The better you get, the more it exposes the insecurity in others. Sometimes the hate doesn't come from the crowd; it comes from the ones you thought were in your corner. And that's when you realize this: If they couldn't break me at my lowest, they'll never break me at my peak.

Those who doubt or ridicule your efforts are naysayers in your story. They're meant to make it interesting. They're watching from the sidelines while you're actively participating on the field. Their role is to hate from the stands, but they don't dictate your path.

Walk with confidence.

And don't let anyone who doesn't know who *they* are tell you who *you* are.

MAXIMIZE YOUR MINDSET

The farther you move along on your journey, the easier it becomes to reach a mindset where other people's opinions don't matter. Too many people get caught up in what others think or say, letting that doubt affect their self-worth and progress.

But here's the reality. Your casket has room for one, not two.

You will die by yourself, so stop living for others.

Nobody's belief in you is more important than your own belief in yourself.

Don't throw away what you've built just because others don't see it.

It's that day you wake up and decide that the only validation you need is your own. That's when you enter the mentality of no return, that mentality of simply not giving a damn.

Who's going to stop you?

The reality is that other people's doubts don't change where you're going unless you let them.

One thing I've always admired about elderly people is that you can see they just don't care, and why should they?

An older man once told me, "I have more years behind me than in front of me, so what do I look like worrying about what people think of me with the little life I have left?"

That message really sat on my heart and gave me further indication that I shouldn't care about what people think or say.

It made me think about my father and how he is unapologetically himself. As a young boy, I always learned from my dad with his actions and not so much from his giving me advice because he is a man of few words. The way my dad has always maneuvered in life is something I've always wanted to adopt in my own life.

Once I started really moving with a free spirit and mind, I started to flourish so much more in my life, and it helped me understand my purpose even more because nothing was clogging or manipulating my mind.

Alright, they
hatin on you, so
what? They don't believe
in you, so what? You gotta stop
lettin the outside noise stop
you from your grind
bro, because
they're the fans
in your story.
They're in the
bleachers for a
reason. You're in
the game. You really
out here in the field.
When you gon stop lettin
nobodies tell you about you?

I do feel that to become a strong leader on a Pure Journey, receiving hate is necessary for your character development. I say that because when you are in the spotlight and so many eyes are on you, you need to know how to take in all those voices that will be speaking to you or at you.

Your ability to block the noise that is trying to pull you from your end goal is a key to Staying Pure because you're not allowing outside noise to pollute your mind. It's the mental toughness that allows you to keep moving forward, even when things get tough or don't go as planned.

Imagine it like walking down a street filled with people. Everyone is hollering and yelling at you, but you truly just can't hear it. That is how you need to approach the opinions of others.

Dial in so hard that it's just you and your journey.

In the beginning, it can feel isolating.

I've been there.

It's hard.

It might just be you and God for a little bit.

But those days don't last forever.

They call it crazy,
I call it focused.
Don't ever let a "sucka"
try to stop you from achieving
your dream. That same
dream that keeps
you up at night.
That same
dream that gets
you emotional
every time that
you think about it.
That same dream that
you know will change your
whole family's life. Yeah, that
one. Don't let no one try to play
you, bro. Go get it.

EVALUATE THE HATE

When people hate on you for no reason with random comments or negative energy, trying to tear you down, it says more about them than it ever will about you.

Not too long ago, we were filming in Puerto Rico, just doing our thing. Some random women started yelling at us. *Who do you think you are? Y'all ain't celebrities!*

We just laughed. We didn't even bother responding to them in any way. We knew the truth.

They weren't mad at us. They were mad at *themselves*. They knew they didn't have the confidence to do what we were doing, and it hit them—hard enough that they had to go out of their way to try to tear us down.

Haters reveal their own insecurity every time they open their mouths. Once you really understand that, you stop getting mad at them. You start feeling sorry for them.

The best thing you can do when hate comes your way is to think before you react.

First, ask yourself, *Is what they're saying even true?*

Usually the answer is no. And once you know it's not true, you know it isn't your reality. It's just noise.

Second, decide this: *Are you going to let this make you or break you?*

Choose to use it. Even if the hate is ridiculous and based on lies or other people's insecurities, let it *make* you. Sometimes you need to add fuel to the fire. When life has been too easy, a little smoke can remind you what you're made of.

Third, be real with yourself. *This is part of the journey.*

They'll say you aren't good enough.

They'll laugh when you fail.

Good.

That means you're doing something worth noticing.

You can't run from it.

You can't be shocked whenever hate shows up. You can't be staring into space, wondering why they said that.

Haters exist.

If they crucified the only perfect man who ever walked the earth, what makes you think you're exempt?

You're not.

I'm not.

It's part of being human.

Don't fold under the scrutiny. Embrace it.

Hate won't stop you.

It just lights the match.

Ultimately, that *Hate Gon' Make You Great.*

PART 3

GET
SUCCESSFUL
OR DIE TRYING

This mindset demands complete dedication to your Pure Journey, no matter the obstacle. It's about pushing through every failure, doubt, and setback because quitting is never an option. I've learned that success doesn't just come from dreaming; it comes from relentless effort, from putting in the work and embracing discomfort. This mentality has forced me to step outside my comfort zone and keep going, even when things feel impossible.

FIND YOUR FLOW

At some point along your Pure Journey, you're going to have to have a revelation—not one that someone just hands you. I mean one that you earn. It's something that hits you in the chest because you've been showing up daily, keeping your promise to yourself. You didn't skip steps. You didn't cheat. You stayed true to the journey.

And one day, you'll feel it. *Click.*

That's what people call a flow state. It's not something you chase. You don't manufacture it. You *become* it.

You step into a rhythm where everything feels aligned. Punctual. Seamless. Like you're not missing a beat. Like your life is moving, not just your days.

I ain't gonna lie,
dawg. It's gonna
have to get to the
point where you wake
up and just say, "I'm the
one. I'm the one that's gonna break
bondage. I'm the one that's gonna create
generational wealth." Plenty
of people are depending
on you, and you're
folding. The
weight is on your
shoulders, bro.

You have a task
at hand every day
that you're not getting
done. People need you,
dawg. And for you just sit
here and be piss poor every
day, knowing that you're the only
person who can make this right, but
you're also the only person who can mess
this up. That's unfair, bro. I need you to
really think about that.

It's all on you.

I first felt it playing basketball. I remember it so clearly, that moment when everything I put up was going in.

I wasn't overthinking.

I wasn't forcing anything.

I was just flowing.

It's like when Steph Curry hits that first shot. Then the second. Then the sixth. People watching think it's talent. But what is it really?

It's trust.

He trusts the work he put in.

He trusts his muscle memory.

He lets go of doubt.

That's what creates the flow state.

And here's the thing no one tells you: That same energy applies off the court too.

It shows up in your work, your health, your relationships, and your spirit. When you're locked in on your routines, your whole life starts to click.

You don't dread tasks.

You don't feel drained all the time.

You're not second-guessing every move.

You're flowing.

But here's the key: You have to keep going, pushing forward, even when it's not flowing, just to get to that point.

You will never hit that rhythm if you quit. Flow doesn't show up for people who keep starting over. It reveals itself to people who stay consistent through the dry seasons.

I remember one time back in eighth grade on a church trip, I was so hungry to feel something real and connect with God in a way that wasn't just talk. I remember asking Pastor Trey, "How do you speak in tongues?"

Pastor Trey looked at me with a smile and said, "You can't force it. You just gotta focus on the Spirit and tune everything else out. It'll come when it comes."

So I locked in. I stopped trying to make it happen. I just surrendered. I let go of every distraction. I focused so hard that I didn't even realize what happened next. I woke up face down on my knees. The lights were on. The band had packed up. Everyone was gone. I was the only one left in the sanctuary.

That's a flow state.

That's what it feels like when you're not pushing. You're just fully present. You're in it so deep that you lose track of time, of pressure, and of people watching. Instead of chasing validation, it's about communion—with God, your journey, and your own grind.

And if I'm being real, it's not just a state of mind. It becomes a way of life.

You hit a groove over a stretch of weeks, then months, where you're waking up on time, hitting your workouts, spending time with your people, honoring your word, and working on your goals.

Not for applause.

Not for likes.

But because you said you would.

That's what I call work momentum.

And here's what most people miss: Work momentum is effort-based, not results-based. When you stack up enough days in flow, the results come. That's when people will say you blew up overnight. But what they didn't see were the days you showed up with no spotlight.

Once the results show up, your motivation gets even stronger because now you're not just dreaming; you're *living* it. That fuels more effort, which fuels more results. And the cycle continues.

This state of mind will have you step in with confidence and declare that you are who you say you are. But carrying that kind of belief, that kind of vision, also comes with weight.

MANAGE YOUR OVERWHELM

Carrying a big vision comes with big pressures. You're not just building for yourself. You're building for the people who look to you for hope. You're the one who can change your family's trajectory. That weight is real, but so is the opportunity.

When you feel overwhelmed, that doesn't mean you're weak. It means you're carrying something heavy. And sometimes the weight isn't a sign you should quit. It's a sign you're on the edge of something major.

You don't have to stay stuck in overwhelm.

You can use it.

You can turn that pressure into power.

Here's how:

- *Shift Your Mindset; This Pressure Is a Privilege*
  You have to decide what pressure means. Is it a curse? Or is it a call?

  Some people see pressure and say, "Why me?"

  Others say, "Why not me?"

  If your people are leaning on you, that's a sign of respect. They see something in you. They believe in your potential, even if you don't always see it yourself.

You don't have to run from that responsibility. You can rise to the occasion. Pressure makes diamonds. It pushes out what's soft and shows you what's solid.

- *Zoom Out and Lay It All Out*
Overwhelm is often just everything crashing into your mind at once. It's like trying to solve a hundred-piece puzzle in your head with no picture.

So step back.

Breathe.

And write everything down.

Don't overthink it. Just dump it all on paper—the deadlines, the worries, the what-ifs, the to-do list that never ends. What happens next might surprise you.

Suddenly, things look smaller. Some problems sink, and others disappear completely. Others reveal themselves as symptoms of a bigger core issue.

That's your target.

Most overwhelm doesn't come from ten different problems. It's one main problem causing ten different symptoms. Find the cause, and you'll regain control.

- *Rank and Attack the Chaos*

Once it's all on the table, sort it. Put things in order. What's the one challenge that would clear the path for everything else once you solve it? That's the nucleus. That's your first domino.

Tackle that one thing first. Focus your energy like a laser.

When I decided to leave the physical therapy assistant program I had enrolled in to follow my passion, I had to weigh what mattered most. Instead of folding under pressure, I stepped back. I owned my decision and embraced the burden of choosing my dream over my safety net.

That took guts. That's how you turn pressure into purpose.

- *Accept the Worst Case and Then Move*
  Sometimes what keeps us stuck is the fear of what might happen. But once you face the worst-case scenario, it loses power.

  Ask yourself this: What's the real consequence if I fail? Will I lose everything or just need to start again? Will I go homeless? Will I die? It's a little extreme, but sometimes you need to ask yourself the wildest consequences just to realize there really isn't a big one from chasing your passion.

  People fail to realize this:

  You can reset.

  You can restrategize.

You can try again.

That's not failure. That's growth.

- *Remind Yourself That This Makes Your Story Better*
  Your life is your story. And what makes a story great?

Adversity.

Turning points.

That moment when the main character backs against the wall and still finds a way forward.

Overwhelm means something is happening. You're in motion. You're building. You're getting tested because you're meant for something more.

You just have to recognize that to figure it out.

So write it down, rank it, attack it, and flip that overwhelm into opportunity.

Embrace the pressure because it's going to develop you. Recognize the critical part you play and take proactive steps every day to fulfill it. Don't let the fear of failure, the pressure, or self-doubt hinder you. Instead, use it as fuel to drive you forward.

BUILD YOUR CONFIDENCE

Self-doubt is one of the biggest killers of dreams. It's the barrier between where you are and where you want to be.

But the truth is, you've been selling yourself short. You've been waiting for someone else to validate what you should already know about yourself.

Confidence is everything, but real confidence comes from within, not from others hyping you up.

When you rely on others for your belief, you give them power over your capabilities.

The key to building confidence is recognizing your value, and that starts with validating yourself. Stop waiting for approval and start taking action. Procrastination is often just another form of self-doubt—it's a way of delaying the inevitable because you don't fully believe in your ability to succeed. But when you stop second-guessing yourself and start taking action, momentum builds.

The journey to confidence begins with small steps. Each small accomplishment will chip away at your self-doubt, and with every success, your belief in yourself will grow. You have to reprogram your mindset.

Change your mindset from "I can't" to "I can, and I will."

Look, I guess I'm gonna be the one to tell you, but stop sleeping on yourself. Because you really been like that. And it shouldn't take some dude on the Internet to tell you that. Why you lacking so much confidence when you're clearly somebody special? Come on, bro, tighten up. I believe in you.

Building confidence starts with eliminating self-doubt, but it doesn't stop there.

No matter how much you practice or know, if you don't believe in yourself, none of it matters. True success begins with the belief that you are capable of achieving your heart's desires.

The moment I found out that the words I speak give life or death was when my mindset went to another level. Belief in yourself is a cheat code to success. Anything you desire is achievable, but it starts with your mindset.

There is genuinely *nothing* you can't do.

The moment you truly believe and see what you are capable of, you unlock a power that fuels your actions.

Real power comes from the understanding that while you can't control everything, you can control your own effort, mindset, and choices.

I first started to develop this mentality when I was very young, playing sports. If you are a current or former athlete, at some point you have been through the politics of that sport. While playing basketball, I witnessed a lot of circumstances that were uncontrollable. Playing time and favoritism are the types of situations that occur, and the only thing you can do as a player is work harder and play better.

I remember I had to make my impact on the court so noticeable that if a coach decided to be unfair, everyone would know it.

GROW FROM YOUR FAILURES

Confidence isn't displayed when everything goes right. It's displayed when you survive what goes wrong.

There was a moment on my journey where I was standing in front of my mom with $600 in my bank account, credit card bills stacking up, and a feeling in my chest like I'd failed. I had invested in my dream, launched my own clothing brand, and taken some hard Ls.

I spent $1,000 on my first drop and sold nothing. I got scammed by a manufacturer in Pakistan and lost another $1,200. And the drop from China? Crickets. I was deep in the red and feeling the weight of every decision pressing down.

But here's the thing. Failure doesn't define you. It *refines* you.

A lot of people get overwhelmed and sit in it. They sulk, they hide, and they feel sorry for themselves. But I couldn't afford that mindset. I didn't need pity. I needed a plan. So I went to someone I trusted—my mom.

We pulled out a journal and got brutally honest. We tracked every dollar in and out. Broke it down to the hour, even what I made at my job for $15 an hour after taxes. That moment wasn't glamorous. It was gritty. But it was also a turning point.

In three months, I went from $600 to $3,500. In ten months, my credit score jumped from 600 to 826. That didn't happen because I got lucky. It happened because I got serious. I stopped avoiding failure and started learning from it.

That's the part people skip over in success stories. They love the highlight reel: my five-figure hoodie drop that sold out, my website crashing from too much traffic, the YouTube video titled *A College Student That Won't Stop Grinding*. But what they don't always see is the grind that didn't work. The nights I doubted myself. The silence after investing my last dollar.

It's easy to trust yourself when things are working. But real confidence is born in the moments when they're not.

I always say you have to learn to lose so you can learn to win.

That's how Michael Jordan did it. He lost to the Pistons year after year. They beat him up, wore him down. So what did he do? He didn't cry about it. He got in the weight room. Got his body right. Came back different, stronger, and more focused. That's exactly what I had to do.

The years 2021 and 2022 were full of losses. In 2023, I came back with wisdom, resilience, and fire.

I learned the hard way that ego is expensive. If you're too proud to ask for help, you'll end up stuck twice as long. That's not strength; it's stubbornness.

When I was overwhelmed, I didn't let pride block my progress. I asked for help. And asking for help isn't weakness; it's wisdom. No one is too good for support. I'd rather get help for a day than struggle for years trying to fix everything alone.

So if you're in a season of loss right now, hear me when I say this: You're not failing; you're training.

Let your setbacks shape you.

Let your mistakes teach you.

Because when you grow from your failure, you stop fearing it.

And when you stop fearing failure, you'll unlock the freedom to win.

CONTROL WHAT YOU CAN CONTROL

Life's gonna throw things at you that you never saw coming. That's a guarantee. A deer could jump in front of your car. Someone might lie to you, steal from you, break your heart, or put you in a situation you didn't ask for.

Anything you
want, you can
get, period. And
you gotta wake up and
tell yourself that every single day.
Look at yourself in the mirror
and tell yourself
what you really
want. You're the
one. And when
you realize that,
boy, I'm telling
you, you're going
to be very powerful.
Because you can control
what you can control. The
world is in your hands. And we're
just waiting to see what you're going
to do with it.

You can't control that.

You can't control the weather, unexpected life events, or what someone else says or does.

But what you can control is *you*.

It starts with your attitude.

With the way you wake up and carry yourself.

How you talk to people.

How you prepare.

Whether you show up on time or come up with excuses.

With your efforts, energy, habits, and choices.

You want peace along your journey? Start here.

Most people stay anxious and frustrated because they spend so much time trying to fix things outside of themselves.

But that's wasted energy. That's a storm you don't need to stand in.

Instead of blaming, start checking yourself. Ask yourself, "What could I have done differently? What can I do right now?"

That's accountability. And that's how you Stay Pure.

If the outcome is always on somebody else and your life is always happening to you, you'll forever be a victim, waiting for the world to change before you do. But if you understand that you are the common denominator, you are the one who's in control, you are the one behind the wheel, then you'll move differently. You'll live with precision.

You'll start doing your due diligence. You'll think twice about the environments you step into, the people you keep nearby, and the moves you make. And that's not fear. That's evolution.

I trust myself more than I trust anybody. It's not that I don't believe in people, but I don't want my life dictated by someone else's choices. If I fail, it's on me. If I miss, it's on me. And when you stop outsourcing your outcomes, that's when you start to grow.

Control what you can control isn't just a phrase. It's a lifestyle, a quiet discipline that compounds over time. When you start living like that, you stop being a victim, wasting time, and giving your power away to things and people who never deserved it in the first place.

And slowly, silently, you become the person you were always meant to be.

GO TO WAR WITH YOURSELF

If you want to evolve on your journey, you've got to kill the version of you that's been killing your future—the one that chooses habit over discipline, excuses over effort, and comfort over greatness. You can't tiptoe around change. You have to be willing to erase the old you and create a new identity.

That war starts in the mirror—not to boost your ego but to be honest.

Call out what's not working.

Your mind is the battlefield. In life, it's rarely your body that gives out. It's your mind telling you, "Stop, this hurts." But if you fight back and say, "Nah, I'm built for this," something shifts. That mindset pushed me past limits I didn't even know I had.

And it doesn't stop. This isn't a one-time transformation; it's a lifelong journey.

Every six months, I check in with myself. That's 180 days to evaluate. What needs to change? What version of myself do I need to bury? Who do I want to become next?

That is how success works. You don't just grow once. You evolve again and again.

Going to war with yourself means letting go of shame and embracing elevation.

The truth is, the world needs the Purest version of you—not the tired, distracted, or reactive version but the real you who got buried under fear and excuses.

So ask yourself, "What do I need to let go of? What do I need to become?"

Answer yourself honestly, and start fighting for it.

And with the work you put in, you're bound to see results, and those results will be the validation you need, not from other people.

You hold the key to your future, and the world is waiting for you to step into your greatness.

DON'T HATE ON NOBODY, AND DON'T WAIT ON NOBODY

The mentality you should have is the *don't hate on nobody and don't wait on nobody* mindset. It's about embodying self-reliance and positivity, and focusing on your own path.

Don't hate on nobody is a mentality that encourages you to release negativity, envy, or resentment toward others.

Wasting energy on hating others only distracts you from your own growth and success.

Instead, focus on celebrating other people's wins and staying rooted on your own journey. Adopting this mindset helps you live with peace, confidence, and a sense of abundance, recognizing that someone else's success doesn't take away from yours.

Don't wait on nobody emphasizes the importance of taking initiative and being proactive. It's a reminder that you are responsible for your own life and progress.

Don't wait for others to validate you, help you, or give you permission to chase your dreams. While support from others can be valuable, your success ultimately depends on your own determination and effort.

Your mentality toward every life scenario can be the determining factor in whether you move yourself forward or backward. Your mind is the most powerful force in existence. If you don't control it, it can destroy you, but if you aren't a slave to it, you have the power to completely transform your life.

Man, I know
sometimes you can
get caught up looking
at other people's success
and looking at what everyone else
is doing, but you gotta be locked into
you, man. Locked into
your own journey.
Know that your
time is going
to come. Know
that you gotta
keep chopping
wood, going brick
by brick, one step
every single day. And
that you're going to be on
top. I know it's hard sometimes
when you climb, you look at people
at the top already where you wanna be,
but you keep pedaling. Just know your
time is coming.

Once you realize your power, you will see that you're more gifted and talented than you think. You have everything it takes to be that 1 percent, but you're *scared*.

I said earlier in the book that avoiding risks gets you nowhere but being a failure.

However, on the opposite side of failure is victory. I have been placed in so many positions where the risk placed in front of me looked so scary.

I had to just trust in God and believe that He would help me execute the way I needed to. At the age of twenty, I was faced with the challenge of having to live on my own and not rely on my parents.

I chose to live on my own because I decided to pursue my passions in life and not take the "safe" route that my parents wanted me to take. I was very frustrated, but I respected the fact that since I wanted to make the choice of foregoing the plans I had made with my parents, I had to be a man and take care of myself.

The reality of that was so scary because at that time I had little income, my savings account was depleted from moving and other unplanned expenses, and it was just an abrupt shift in my life.

I was selling shoes, laptops, clothes—trying anything to make a quick buck to pay my rent. I felt really hopeless.

You know you could
be the one if you
really wanted to, right? You
know that, right? But you keep
playing the what-if game. What if it
don't work out this? What
if it don't work out
that? But what if it
do? What if it do
work out? Then
what? You gonna
be happy, right?
You can't say you
wanna win, but then
you scared to lose.
What kind of sense does
that make? If you put your
head down and lock in on the
vision, how could you not win? Only
thing that's gonna cause you to lose is

your mentality.

But one day I just looked myself in the mirror and said, "If the path I was taking was easy, everyone would do it," and from there I put my head down and locked in on the mission. The rest of that year, I heavily pursued my passions while finishing my degree online and working forty-hour shifts at a local retail store. I had a lot of nights where I would get only four hours of sleep, and I was running on E, but I just really wanted it.

I wasn't going to let the fear of failing consume me, and I was determined to do everything I could to make it work.

I need you to believe in yourself and break out of this mentality that you have.

I had it too.

But that's the mentality that will kill any ounce of chance you have to make it.

I realized that the loss I could take wouldn't be bigger than the win I could take.

With the gifts and abilities God has given you, it's impossible for you to lose if you don't stop.

Stop getting in your own head and hindering yourself to your potential.

You need to develop the mentality to treat success like an obligation, not a choice.

You need to have the energy that you will *Get Successful or Die Trying.*

PART 4

TOUGH TIMES BUILD TOUGH PEOPLE

Tough times are the crucible that shapes you. They don't break you; they refine you. The adversity you face reveals the strength within you, and each challenge is a lesson in resilience. When life tests you, it's not about whether you can endure but how you rise from it. Tough times didn't break me; they shaped me into someone I've always imagined.

Let's talk about what *tough* means because there's a big difference between *looking* tough and *being* tough.

Looking tough is a facade. It's a mask you put on when you're trying to hide how lost or afraid you feel. You might have the mean mug, the silence, or the front, but underneath all that, you're unsettled. When you set out to *act* strong, that probably means you don't trust yourself to actually *be* strong.

Real toughness is deeper.

Pure toughness is about being honest with yourself about where you're at and still moving forward. The toughness lies when life isn't going your way and you still choose to get up and go after it the next day. It's about staying grounded even when life tries to knock you off your pivot. Toughness means you're willing to feel what you're feeling without letting it define your actions. It means you can sit with the pain, uncertainty, and disappointment without folding.

On a normal day, toughness shows up in small ways. It's the discipline to stick to your routine. It's doing what you said you would, even when nobody's watching. It's staying locked in even when results haven't been showing. I always say if you can't stay locked in when things are easy, you're not gonna suddenly become locked in when things get hard.

But reality is when the unexpected happens, when adversity shows up. That's when your toughness and mentality get tested. And by then, it's too late to build it from scratch.

You either trust yourself or you don't.

Picture this: The foundation of your body is your legs. Now imagine someone tries to push you. If your base is strong, you don't budge. That's what mental toughness looks like when life throws its worst at you. You're getting hit, but you're still standing. You aren't rattled. You don't fold.

And folding is a decision.

It's always interesting how hyped people are at the beginning of their journey.

You're excited. Motivated. Locked in.

You talk about the goals you're going to achieve, the dreams you're going to chase, and how nothing's going to stop you.

But then reality sets in.

And that energy disappears.

That's when you find out who's built for this.

Man, what happened to all that
energy you had, all
that ambition,
all that focus
you said you
were going
to have?
But you're
folding. But that's
between you and
you. Hope you can live
with that.

I call it "capping" when people say all the things they're going to do but don't follow through. They let the pressure deflate them and expose who they really are. They start folding the moment the weather changes. And listen, it's easy to look focused when life is calm. It's when the storm hits that we find out if we are who we say we are.

Pure strength is quiet, resilient, and poised.

You don't have to talk about your potential when you're out here living it. And when it gets hard?

That's when you double down and accept what's being thrown your way.

That's when you remember who you said you wanted to be.

And that's when you show yourself that you're not folding.

A LIVING EXAMPLE

When I think of someone who embodies Pure toughness, I think of my older brother.

He's been through more adversity than most people would ever guess, but I've never seen him fold—not once. He's never made excuses, even when the situation would have completely justified it. He just accepts the hand he's been dealt and plays it with purpose.

I watched him go through it firsthand when he was working on getting into medical school. It was 2020, and he was down to his last few prerequisites. There was a chemistry class he had to pass with a certain score, and it kept tripping him up. He was just a point or two away from the score he needed—*twice*. That's how close he was. So many people would have walked away at that point, told themselves it wasn't meant to be, and picked a different route.

Not my brother.

He just looked at the results, shook his head, and said, "Alright, we run it back again."

No quitting.

No detour.

No pity party.

He was working at a hospital at the time—training people, paying for his school and rent, and keeping himself afloat. Even after those long days and longer nights, he found the strength to hit the books and go again—not just to pass but to excel. In his mind, doing the bare minimum isn't tough. He shows up with excellence. Every time.

Even after he made it into medical school, the challenges kept coming. He enrolled in a FLEX program that required flying out every other weekend to Texas for labs and tests. For four years he's been studying to become a doctor while working multiple jobs—still training, still grinding, and still holding himself to that same impossible standard.

People told him not to work during med school because it was too much and would burn him out. But he didn't care what was recommended. He didn't let the limitations others set on themselves be his reality. He had a vision and was willing to dig deep to see it become a reality.

Even when the workload got too heavy and his grades started slipping, his response wasn't "Let me quit this job" or "Let me drop out." It was "How can I get better at scheduling my time so I can still excel?"

That's Pure toughness.

It's showing up even when the circumstances aren't perfect—adjusting, refining, and refusing to let anything knock you off your pivot.

Back in college, he was chasing his basketball dream. He worked so hard that he ended up with severe shin splints in both legs. The doctors told him that if he kept pushing, he could break both legs. That should have been crushing news, but it didn't wreck him. He listened to the doctors, took the L in stride, and kept moving forward.

He switched majors from engineering to exercise science. And from there, he doubled down on becoming a doctor.

He's a DACA student too. If you know what that means, then you know the challenges and limits that come with it. But you'd never hear him use it as a reason to stop.

He's motivated by more than personal success. He wants to *impact the world*. He built his own fitness app and is currently working on another one specifically for the medical field. He has ideas and innovations that can truly change the way healthcare works.

All that is possible because of the way he handles pressure.

That's what makes my brother the toughest man I know.

Not because he talks a big game.

Not because he's never struggled.

But because *he never lets the struggle win.*

YOU WEREN'T MADE TO FOLD

Folding under pressure happens. It's happened to me. It's happened to you. We've all folded at some point. But the question isn't if you've ever folded. It's whether you're willing to admit it.

Essentially, when you're folding, you're letting yourself down.

Folding isn't always weakness. Sometimes it's burnout, fear, or confusion. But most times, it's a lack of trust in yourself.

And if you can't count on you, no one can.

Trusting yourself is the foundation for everything. The reason people fold more often than not is because deep down they don't believe they'll follow through. They don't trust their own words. So they talk big, but their actions don't echo what they say.

Trust is a muscle you can build.

You don't magically wake up and believe in yourself. You earn that belief by keeping the small promises to yourself on a daily basis—like getting up when you said you would, doing the work when nobody's watching, and following through when quitting would be easier.

Start small.

Start somewhere.

But start.

Make a mental contract with yourself. Break it down. If waking up at 7:00 feels too hard, wake up at 8:00. Master that and then level up. Every time you follow through, you're stacking proof that you can count on yourself.

Folding is about deciding if you're willing to stay down after you hit the ground. It's whether you lie to yourself about giving it your all when deep down you know you haven't. If that's you, decide right now to let that go.

Don't waste your time beating yourself up about folding. All that matters is what you do next.

Accept it.

Learn from it.

Then adjust your approach so it doesn't happen again.

I recently told myself that I would stream every single day. And after doing it for seven to eight hours a day for weeks, I could feel myself hitting a wall. I got sick. I felt weak, and I had to take a break.

So technically, yeah, I folded.

But I didn't lie to myself about it.

I was honest. I took the L, made a better plan, and got back up.

The key is to reignite that energy.

Remember why you started in the first place.

Don't let temporary setbacks or distractions pull you away from what's really important. You owe it to yourself to stay focused and follow through on the promises you made to yourself.

Get back up, refocus, and prove to yourself that you're not going to fold when things get tough.

Some things go
wrong just so it can go
right. These Ls are not losses;
they're lessons. This hardship is
meant to make you,
not break you.
So don't be out
here quitting
because you
don't know
where the lesson's
gonna take you. All
soldiers go through
war. Just make sure you
keep your head up and come out
on top.

You weren't meant to lose; you're meant to learn.

You're meant to face it, feel it, and fight through it. So if you've fallen short, forgive yourself but keep pedaling forward.

Come back better, smarter, and even tougher than before.

The next version of you is built from everything that tried to break you but didn't.

WELCOME TO THE WALL – NOW PUSH THROUGH

On your journey, things might occur that you won't understand at the present time.

However, you're being set up for a major victory. Challenges and setbacks aren't just obstacles; they're opportunities for growth. What might seem like a loss is actually a lesson in disguise meant to teach you and build you up rather than tear you down.

The key is to change your perspective on failure. Instead of seeing difficulties as reasons to give up, view them as important parts of your journey. Each challenge provides valuable insights that guide you toward future success. Remember, every struggle has the potential to shape you into a stronger, wiser individual—and ultimately who you need to be.

Embrace those moments as crucial learning experiences. Have a competitive mentality that views them as a challenge you have to conquer. The important thing is not to quit just because you can't immediately see the benefits of the challenge. Stay committed to the process, knowing that every hardship brings you closer to your ultimate goal.

Every successful person embodies three key traits: they face challenges, show resilience to overcome setbacks, and demonstrate diligence to stay committed to their goals. Your journey is a unique process of transformation, and every step, whether easy or challenging, is purposeful.

No one is excused from challenges. I don't care who you are or where you came from. You're gonna go through something. Everybody has their own battles. Some people hide it better than others, but it's there. You might not see it coming, and you might not be ready for it. But your next challenge is coming regardless. How are you gonna show up when you have to look your challenges in the eye? That's what separates people.

Then there's resilience. People throw it around all the time. It's like riding a bike uphill with the wind pushing hard against you. You're tired, your legs are burning, and it feels like you're stuck in the same place.

But you keep pedaling.

You don't stop.

Even if you're only moving an inch a day, you're still moving. That's resilience. That's how I live—clocking in to myself every single day, no matter what. Whether it's a good day or a bad day, I pedal forward. Getting 1 percent better is still a win.

Diligence is when you apply intensity to discipline. You're bringing pure drive to your goal every day, even when nobody's watching, the results aren't visible, or you feel like quitting. That's diligence. You can't be passive when you're diligent. You move like your purpose is on the line—because it is.

Things might happen that feel unfair or difficult to comprehend in the moment, but trust that those experiences are preparing you for something greater. Life's challenges and setbacks are not roadblocks; they are steppingstones designed to build your character, sharpen your skills, and prepare you for the victories ahead. And it's during the hardest moments of your journey that those traits are truly put to the test.

Just letting you know
that when times get tough,
we get to see who's really built for
this. And I ain't gonna
lie to you, bro, I
know your back
is against the
wall, but this is
where we want
you though. Cause
I know you made out
of something special,
and I know you can do it.

When life gets hard, that's when your true self shows up. Anybody can stay strong and positive when things are easy, but who are you when times are tough?

LESSON LEARNED

Tough times are when you separate yourself from the rest of the pack. That is where you get to see your strength and resilience, or your lack thereof. For me, anytime I've gone through hardship, I always address it with a mentality that allows me to see the positive in it.

I remember a while ago I had a Tesla, and during the summer, the screen cracked due to the intense heat and sunlight. If you know anything about Teslas, you know it's a pretty hefty price to fix the screen. So naturally, I put off getting it fixed. During that time, the cracked screen started causing a few issues. Similar to an iPhone with a cracked screen, it began acting on its own, randomly pressing buttons. But here's the kicker: The Tesla screen kept blasting the AC for long periods of time, which drained the battery. And it only happened while I was driving.

One night I left my office, opened the door to my Tesla, and was hit with freezing cold air. There was water on the windows from the AC running nonstop. The worst part was that my battery was at 0 percent. I was totally befuddled. I knew I still had a few miles to go before I reached the charging station, but my car was stuck going no faster than 30 miles per hour, and I was genuinely worried it would just shut off at any moment.

My nerves were on edge, and I was praying to God that I'd make it there.

Somehow, I managed to get to the charging station, only for my Tesla to completely shut off as I pulled into the parking spot. I couldn't believe it. The car was dead. Nothing worked. I couldn't close the windows, open the door, or even get the charging port to open.

I was heartbroken and discouraged by what had just happened. The cost of replacing the battery in a Tesla is enough to buy two used 2010 Hondas. I stayed at the charging station for two hours, just trying to figure out what I was going to do next.

When I got home, my brother was in the kitchen, just nodding his head and smiling at me. I obviously wasn't in the mood for any of that. My mom had already told him what had just happened to me, and he had the look of someone who was happy for me.

He told me, "It's gonna be alright, bruh, this is what you need." He said that this was a setback, but he told me this is a reason for me to go harder and come out stronger than I ever was. As he was talking to me, my discouragement and anger were slowly disappearing, and I realized he was right. My back was against the wall, and I needed to figure out how to handle it.

Pressure is a privilege, the privilege to see if you're made of the right stuff and be clutch in times of trouble. Having my brother instill that confidence in me really shifted my mentality, and I snapped back into a survival mindset instead of a pity mindset.

The point is, when you're faced with challenges, don't see them as setbacks; see them as opportunities to prove what you're truly capable of. It may feel like you're out of options, like you're stuck. But that's exactly where you need to be.

Pressure doesn't exist to destroy you; it exists to push you beyond what you thought was possible. In moments of desperation, you find strength and clarity. It's when you have no other option but to fight that you realize how much power you actually have.

Embrace that pressure because that's what makes winners. You were chosen for this path because you have the strength, vision, and drive to succeed where others can't. You owe it to yourself to push forward. We can't prepare for what life throws at us, but we have to be ready to embrace the test we receive.

Don't get thrown off your pivot.
Life's gonna throw a lot of
things at you, but
it's supposed to
happen. It's
supposed to test
your character.
Adversity builds
the strongest
warriors. And I believe
you're one of the strongest
warriors out.

THE PAYOFF IS GREATER THAN THE PAIN

Most people miss the beauty in life's challenges. I get it. It's hard to appreciate the lesson when you're still sitting in it. But if you take a step back, you'll see what I mean. Every setback, every delay, and every disappointment is there to develop you.

If you're really about this Pure Journey, then you need to understand that your struggles aren't random. They're custom-designed to prepare you for the purpose God put you here to fulfill. That's why the strength you develop from passing these tests is the kind that stays with you.

It's unwavering.

It's embedded.

You can't buy it or fake it.

You earn it by showing up when life hits hard.

When you pass through hard seasons, you're building character, and that's the one thing nobody can take away from you.

So how do you hold onto that strength once the storm passes? Keep the habits that built you. If the adversity forced you to get up early, stay disciplined. If it made you pray more, journal more, or save more, don't stop just because things look easy now. Let that structure and discipline become part of your DNA.

Tough times don't stop coming.

And if you made it through once, you can do it again.

That's why I journal.

In my lowest moments, I wrote everything down—my credit score, my bank account, my thoughts. I go back and read those pages as a reminder that I've been through worse and made it. It builds my composure and keeps me poised when life tries to rattle me again.

Eventually, you stop fearing the storm.

You stop panicking when the pressure shows up.

You start thinking, "Alright, let's run it back. I've done this before. Let's see what I'm made of this time."

That's the *dawg* mentality. You stop dodging every adversity and start meeting it head on.

The payoff of staying tough is transformation. You get to the other side of the storm with more grit, clarity, and capacity to handle what's next.

You level up.

And if you're locked in during the hard times, the strength becomes part of you.

If you're in a storm right now, remember this: You weren't meant to be regular.

You were built for something greater.

And every obstacle you're facing is just part of the process that proves it.

Because *Tough Times Build Tough People.*

PART 5

THE PURE GIFT YOU CAN'T RECLAIM

It's the purest gift you'll ever receive, yet it's the one you can't hold onto. We often treat it as if it's endless, wasting moments we think we can relive later. But once time slips away, it's gone for good. There's no going back, no do-overs. Every second is an opportunity that you can choose to invest in or let pass. The true power of time lies in how you use it and the choices you make in every fleeting moment. It's a gift that's meant to be treasured, for it shapes the life you'll live and the person you'll become. In the end, the question isn't whether you had enough time but whether you used it to build something meaningful and something lasting. Your time is yours, but it's limited. Make it count.

Imagine your life as an hourglass, each grain of sand slipping through, one by one, never to return. Time is the purest gift you'll ever receive yet the one thing you can never get back.

It's constant, relentless, and unmoved by your excuses. It doesn't care if you need more, whether you're ready or not. That ticking clock isn't just background noise; it's a reminder that every moment matters.

And yet how often do we spend our days waiting for the right moment?

You gotta run the day or the day will run you.

You're waiting as if time's gonna slow down and wait on you.

See, look the
clock is ticking,
the clock never stops
ticking, time don't wait for
nobody. So why you sitting
here wasting your
day away
thinking that
you deserve
tomorrow when
you're playing
with today? That's
crazy. Until you
realize that you're wasting
your life away and that you're
not gonna be able to get this time
back, you're just setting yourself up
for failure.

But here's what I need you to understand: Every second you waste thinking you've got time is a second that's gone. This is the one thing we spend without even realizing it's being spent.

Once it's gone, you can't refund, redo, or reclaim it.

The most valuable thing I spent time on this year was building my content and my brand, and writing this book. And I'm not just saying that because you're reading it now. This year alone, I spent somewhere between 3,500 and 4,000 hours creating, editing, learning, and pouring into my craft. That's more time than people spend at a full-time job in a year by almost double.

But here's the thing: Investing all that time didn't bring me money.

Not yet.

So you might be wondering how I can say it was *valuable*.

It's because value isn't always measured in dollars. Sometimes it's measured by the foundation you're establishing. Every hour I put into my content and my message is a brick laid for what I'm building for the long term, and everything else I do will stand on that.

I see it like a job interview. Every post, every word, every message is a representation of me. For a lot of people, it's their first impression of who I am. So I take it seriously. I put in the hours because I believe in the impact it will have in the future.

Understand this: Every day is a blank canvas. Every action is a brushstroke. Your masterpiece is built on the small, consistent movements. It's how you spend the hours no one else sees—the nights, the mornings, the in-betweens—because wasted time never returns.

And when you treat time like the rare, nonrenewable resource it is, you move with urgency, not anxiety. You stop running from time and start carving your mark into it.

At the end of your life, no one's gonna talk about how many likes you had, how much money you had, or how clean your Instagram layout was. They're gonna talk about who you were, what you did with your time, and who you became because of it.

So take the risk while you still have the hours.

Start before the clock runs out.

Wake up early and claim the time others waste.

Learn the skill that will outlive you.

Chase the dream because tomorrow isn't promised.

You only get one life. Make sure it counts.

See, your
problem is that
you keep rushing the
process; you ain't trying to
be patient. Good things come to those
who wait. This ain't a sprint, this is
a marathon. And the
more you keep
worrying about
the future, the
more you're
gonna get lost
in the present.
You gotta get up
and just put one
foot in front of the
other bruh, and just have
that blind faith. But what I
will say is that we don't know
when it's happening, but we know
it's coming. We ain't putting this work
in for no reason.

DON'T FALL FOR THE TRAP OF MICROWAVE SUCCESS

The world we live in makes it really easy to want things fast. You see people post their highlights, and it starts to feel like you're behind. I call it microwave success when you want the results without putting in real work. You want the blessing without the lesson, the glory without the grind.

If you're only focused on where you're trying to go, you'll miss the importance of where you are right now.

I've felt that impatience in myself. Early on, I'd watch someone blow up and get opportunities and wonder, *Man, when's it gonna be my turn?*

But then I reminded myself that everyone's journey is different.

I don't know what God's doing in their life, and I don't know what He's still preparing in mine. Some people get a taste of success early because they need it more than you do. Maybe God's building their confidence or helping them survive. I've come to believe that God knows what each of us can handle and when we're ready for it.

When I think about staying grounded in the middle of all that, one quote always comes to mind—LeBron James in

2011. After he left Cleveland and joined the Miami Heat, the world expected an instant championship.

But they lost that first year.

And what did he say? "Rome wasn't built in a day."

He was right.

They needed to put the pieces together, build chemistry, and go through the fire together.

And the next year, they won it all.

Just because something isn't happening right now doesn't mean it won't happen later. And just because you're not seeing the results yet doesn't mean the work isn't working.

You didn't just wake up one day and become the person you are. You've been shaped by experiences, choices, Ls, and Ws.

It's all a process.

And if you stay committed to getting 1 percent better each day, over time you'll look back and realize how far you've come.

That's why I always say, *Today is the best I've ever been, but it's the worst I'll ever be.*

I'm not done growing. I know I'll be better tomorrow, not because of luck but because I'm committed to showing up and putting in the work every day.

We live in a fast world. But there is no fast track to success. You have to build it brick by brick.

If you're only chasing quick wins, you'll burn out when things get tough because you haven't developed any mental endurance or foundation. Your mind can't even fathom working toward something that doesn't happen overnight. If you're in it for the long game, you'll weather the storms, grow stronger, and walk in the kind of purpose that can't be taken from you.

Stay grounded and trust the process.

The reward is coming.

YOU NEED TWO KINDS OF FAITH

It's not about knowing how every single thing is going to turn out. It's about trusting yourself and the work you're putting in. That's where blind faith comes in. You don't need all the answers right now; you just need the determination and diligence to keep moving forward, even when things aren't perfect. That blind faith comes from your true belief in yourself. And that belief is developed from showing up for yourself day in and day out.

But you're gonna need more than blind faith sometimes. You also need *delusional* faith. And yeah, I know how that sounds. Let me break it down.

Blind faith is when you're in the middle of the grind, working hard every day, and you don't see any visible progress. Nothing seems to be clicking. But you keep going anyway.

Deep down, you believe it's going to pay off. You trust that it's coming; you just don't know when or how. You just know there's a light at the end of the tunnel.

That's how I live.

Tomorrow just might be the day.

And if it isn't?

Cool. Maybe it's the next day.

That mindset is what keeps me going. It's the possibility of a breakthrough.

Delusional faith is different.

It's when you believe in something so big, so unlikely, that it doesn't make any logical sense, and you believe it anyway. You've got no evidence. No blueprint. No stats to back you up. But something in you still says, "Nah, I'm still going to make it happen." The thought of you thinking you're any different than someone else chasing the same thing is actually delusional because honestly, what makes you so special?

It was delusional. But it happened. It happened because I believed it before I saw it, even though it made absolutely no sense. Delusional faith means that I think the odds don't apply to me. It might not work for someone else, but it will certainly work for me.

It's not rooted in proof. It's rooted in vision.

Here's the reality: You're the first *you* who has ever existed. Nobody's lived your life before you. There's no case study to follow. So of course it's going to look crazy when you believe in a future that's never been seen before. But you need that kind of delusion. That kind of belief is the seed of every breakthrough.

Here's how I see it: Blind faith is for when you're deep in the journey, doing the reps, with no results to show for it, but you're too committed to stop. Delusional faith is what gets you started in the first place, especially when nobody else believes in your vision. It's the gas in the tank before you even hit the road.

I know some of you struggle with doubt. I get it. Life can throw a lot at you. But if you can lean into both kinds of faith, you're going to get there.

I think the question you should ask yourself is this: Do you believe in yourself? *For real?*

That's what all this comes down to. You have to believe it before it happens and then work like it's already yours.

ESTABLISH YOUR OWN MAMBA DRILLS

One of my favorite basketball players, Kobe Bryant, is a perfect example of the type of mindset we all need to tap into. If you know anything about the late great Kobe Bryant, you know he embodied consistency. He had specific routines he did every day, over and over again, until those moves became second nature.

No hesitation. No doubt.

That's what made him unstoppable. He knew that repetition creates confidence, and confidence creates freedom. He wasn't wondering if the shot would fall. He *knew* it would because he had already made that shot 1,000 times in practice before ever stepping on the court for a game.

When I think about getting 1 percent better every day and being consistent, Kobe is who always comes to mind. No matter what, he promised himself he would give his all to his craft every day, and it resulted in his being one of the greatest basketball players to ever play.

I've got my own version of Mamba drills now.

For me, it's simple routines that lock me in. I start with prayer. I journal. I stretch. I eat the same stuff almost every day.

Some people might say that's boring, but to me, it's freeing. It means I'm not wasting mental energy on decisions that really don't matter. That energy gets redirected into what does matter.

My purpose.

My business.

My craft.

My growth.

Even the way I organize my space is part of it. It's not untidy; everything is right where I want it. I'd feel lost if something got moved. That's how disciplined and deeply embedded my routine is. And I get a lot of it from my dad. He's the most structured person I know. It's just in our DNA.

Back when I was twenty, I entered into a lifestyle I called *robot mode*. I built out a block schedule for every part of my life. It went something like this: Wake up at this time, eat this, study here, edit there, have a snack—you get the idea. I was on that strict routine for five months, and it changed my life.

After a while, I didn't need to look at the schedule anymore. My body and mind just knew what to do. It became instinctual. And that's the point. Once the routine becomes second nature, you've cleared out the space in your head to start thinking bigger. You're no longer just surviving the day; you're advancing.

That is why you need your own Mamba drills.

You don't need to copy mine or anyone else's. Figure out what your pillars are and then do them over and over and over.

I've got fifteen things on my to-do list on a light day and twenty-five to thirty when it's packed. They aren't all massive goals. Some are simple like calling this person, replying to that email, running this errand, brainstorming.

Why?

Because it's the small things that get forgotten. And the small things that are done consistently create massive results.

The trick is that once something becomes automatic, it's no longer taking energy from you; it's giving it back. You're not negotiating with yourself anymore. You're not asking, "Should I go to the gym today?" It's already decided. That's just who you are.

What are the non-negotiables in your day that keep you locked in?

What routines do you need to create so you're no longer questioning your greatness but proving it to yourself daily?

I believe in you, but the real question is this: *Do you believe in yourself enough to keep going?*

Build your steps. And climb them every single day.

MAKE THE MOST OF YOUR TIME

You can't afford to waste time on things that don't align with your life. You can't keep handing hours away to people, distractions, or habits that aren't feeding your growth. Making the most of your time doesn't have to be perfect. It starts with awareness and being honest with yourself about where you are and where your time is really going.

POINT OUT THE DISTRACTIONS

Before you can limit distractions, you have to call them out. What's really pulling you away from the work? For me, it's my phone and other people, not even in a bad way but just in conversations. I find myself conversing way too long, and then boom, an hour's gone.

That's why the first thing you need to do is build some accountability with yourself.

Ask this:

- What's consistently taking me off track?

- Is this a controllable or uncontrollable situation?

If it's uncontrollable, like your home environment or something out of your hands, you've got to create a system around it. Maybe that means studying at the library instead of at home or putting your phone on Do Not Disturb and getting out of the house for a few hours. Whatever it is, find a space where you can lock in.

If it's controllable, then it's time for some cold-turkey energy. Cut it off. No negotiation. If streaming seasons of shows is the issue, cancel the subscription. If it's a relationship that's draining your time without building you up, leave the situation. If you're serious about your goals, you've got to make serious and punctual moves.

CREATE A DAILY RHYTHM

I've said it before—robot mode changed everything for me. I don't follow it as strictly now, but that structure built the discipline I still lean on today.

If you're trying to reclaim your time, start with a consistent daily routine. Include these types of non-negotiables:

- Prayer or meditation

- Physical movement or stretching

- Breaks that recharge you

- Time for reflection or journaling

When your day has rhythm, you're not wasting time deciding what comes next; you're just flowing throughout your day. That mental clarity is important.

PROTECT YOUR YES
BY SAYING NO

One of the biggest time traps people fall into is not knowing when or how to say no. I'm not talking about peer pressure or negative influences. Sometimes it's as simple as a friend texting, "Yo, you tryna hoop at 8:30?"

As much as I'd love to, if I know that time needs to be spent on editing content or packaging orders, then the answer has to be no. It's not because I don't want to hang but because I'm choosing what matters most.

You've got to ask yourself this: Am I trading what I want *most* for what I want *right now*?

That little question will put everything in perspective.

Every time you say no to something that doesn't serve your goals, you're saying yes to your future. And on the flip side, every yes you give without intention is a no to something that could have pushed you closer to your breakthrough.

START WHERE YOU ARE

You don't have to overhaul your whole life overnight. Just start paying attention. Start keeping it real with yourself. Write down your distractions. Build a simple routine. Protect your energy.

Time will pass.

Whether you use it wisely or not is on you.

Stop handing your time to things that don't deserve it.

You've got work to do. Let's get after it.

YOU DON'T HAVE TIME TO LIVE IN FEAR

Time and fear are deeply connected because fear often drives how we perceive and use our time. Fear of failure, fear of missing out, or fear of making the wrong choice can make us hesitant, causing us to delay action or overthink decisions, ultimately wasting precious time. This hesitation stems from the uncertainty of outcomes, leading us to wait for a "perfect moment" that won't ever arrive.

You get one
chance at life, bro.
You don't get to redo
this over again. You can't
afford to be scared because if you die
tomorrow, then what? I'd rather be on my
deathbed knowing I lived the
life I wanted to live.
I did the things I
wanted to do, and
I'm content with
it. You can't be
on your deathbed
saying like, "Hey,
I wish I would've
done this." What are
you scared for? Why are
you scared to put in work? Why
are you scared to change your life?
You're scared of success. That makes
no sense. How are you gonna be scared of
something that has high reward, even the
risk like what's the risk? So what? It didn't
work out. Like life goes on.

Fear has the power to define your entire life. It can either push you toward greatness or hold you captive, keeping you from ever reaching your true potential.

It's that invisible barrier that holds you back.

It whispers in your ear, whispers doubt, exaggerates the consequences of failure, and convinces you that staying in your comfort zone is safer than stepping out into the unknown.

Truth be told, being comfortable and staying where you're at is far more of a risk than actually taking the chance at something.

Not knowing what your life could have been or who you could have been is a scary reality. The unknown is not something you want to die with.

What people fail to realize is that you only have one shot at life, and your goal is to seek all the answers pertaining to your purpose.

On your deathbed, you don't want to think, "What if I had done this?" or "What if I had done that?" because that will eat at your spirit, knowing you let yourself down, and ultimately leave you with regret.

I'd rather take the leap and face the possibility of failure than let fear keep me wondering forever about what could have been.

Don't let that be you.

Take a chance on yourself. You owe it to yourself to discover who you're truly meant to become.

Your fear might be the one thing you need to overcome in order to stop wasting time, which is *the Pure Gift You Can't Reclaim.*

PART 6

CUTTING TIES AND BUILDING BRIDGES

The hardest part of growth is knowing what to let go of. We get so comfortable in our lifestyle and our ways of thinking that they become like chains we carry with us, even when they no longer serve us. The real breakthrough happens when you have the courage to cut those invisible ties, the ones that kept you anchored in the past. To truly move forward, you must start building bridges. Those aren't just connections with others but with new opportunities, new ways of thinking, and the version of yourself that's waiting on the other side.

STOP CAPPING

A "capper" is a person you should never want to be. It is the person who writes checks they can never cash. A capper makes empty promises, especially to themselves.

Here's the thing. At first, it sounds good. You tell people, "I'm about to start this business" or "I'm getting in the gym this month" or "This year I'm locked in." But they're just words. You aren't actually doing anything. That's capping.

We've all done it. I'm not gonna act like I'm above it. I've had seasons where I found myself saying what sounds good but not taking action. I'd talk about what I was gonna do, but in reality, I was dragging my feet.

Hey, look at this person right here. This the one who talks about all the things they're gonna do but don't do it. This the one who always tells everybody that they're gonna do this by the end of the year but never completes it. This is the capper. You tired of that label? Do something about it.

The reason you just talk about what you're going to do is because you like that little dopamine rush that comes with the words. It feels like progress even when you haven't moved an inch.

Here's where it gets real. That habit will kill your momentum.

The more you do it, the more you start to lose trust, not just from the people around you but from *yourself.*

And when you stop trusting yourself, you stop believing that your words mean anything.

Let me ask you this:

- How many times have you told someone (or yourself) that you were gonna do something and didn't?

- How many times have you hyped up a new season, plan, or version of yourself, but nothing changed?

- How many times have you said you were done procrastinating but kept pushing it off?

Be real. Look in the mirror. Is that you?

Because if it is, it's time for a wake-up call.

You're damaging your reputation with others, but more importantly, you're damaging your relationship with your own potential.

And trust me, people start to notice.

The more you cap, the more people stop taking you seriously.

Eventually, every time you say you're gonna do something, folks just think, "Yeah, right. I'll believe it when I see it."

That's not the energy you want around your name.

My dad taught me something I'll never forget. When you live with integrity, rumors don't stick.

People won't believe lies about you if your actions consistently speak for you. That's the reputation I work to build. I say I'm gonna do something, and I do it. Period.

So if you're tired of being someone who talks more than they move, you've got to cut that tie right now. Let go of the ego boost that comes from saying the thing and start chasing the discipline that comes from actually doing it instead.

Capping is easy.

Execution is rare.

Which one you choose says everything about who you're becoming.

LIMIT YOUR DEPENDENCE

Being a dependent person can destroy you.

All some people know is the feeling of dependency, and they live life with an entitlement that does nothing but hurt them.

You want to get screwed over?

Start depending on other people.

Why would you even want your situation to be in the hands of someone else?

You need to depend on yourself because you're all you've got.

I'm not saying that having a team is an issue, but having the mindset as if someone is supposed to do something for you or the mindset of relying on someone as if you're helpless is a predicament you should never be in.

Go learn and find out how to get it done.

At the end of the day, you need to assume that people do not care, even if they do.

The reality is that humans don't care about you more than they do themselves, so you have to be your own backbone.

The world doesn't
owe you anything and
people shouldn't feel sorry
for you. You gotta be the person
that takes matters into
your own hands
and go get it.
No one's gonna
grind for you,
no one's gonna
win for you, no
one's gonna get in
your casket with you,
no one's gonna buy your
house, no one's gonna take care
of your family for you. That's your
responsibility and you know it.

My parents always raised me to be an independent person and do everything in my power to figure out things on my own. It's helped me a lot, and it's given me a lone wolf or survival mentality, if you will.

I remember when I was a freshman in college and living on my own. I loved the independence that came with that. A lot of seventeen- or eighteen-year-olds are hesitant or less likely to live on their own, which in this specific circumstance is okay.

But the point I'm really making is that when it was time for me to truly depend on myself and not have Mom and Dad be there at my disposal to help me figure out day-to-day decisions, I didn't run from it.

When you depend on others to carry you, you're giving away your control and setting yourself up for disappointment.

No one is obligated to save you, and the sooner you realize that, the stronger you are and more prepared.

It's not about rejecting help; it's about knowing that help should be a bonus, not a necessity. When you build your foundation on self-reliance, you create something unshakable.

No one can take away what you've built because it's not dependent on others for validation or support. It's something you've crafted through your own effort, discipline, and vision. Self-reliance gives you the ability to stand firm in the face of adversity because you know that what you've achieved is a direct result of your own choices, decisions, and actions.

In a world where circumstances and people can change, what you've built for yourself is untouchable. It becomes a testament to your perseverance, independence, and unwavering commitment to your goals.

With that commitment, you will inevitably become a winner.

USE YOUR DISCERNMENT TO MAKE NECESSARY CUTS

But the question is this: What are you willing to sacrifice to win?

Many people are in love with the idea of winning, but when it's time to put the necessary action toward winning, they don't give up habits that are prohibiting them.

We all have habits, some good and some bad, but what most people don't realize is that our bad habits are what silently sabotage success. You're only getting in your own way. It might be procrastination, distractions, or even negative thinking, but whatever it is, it's time to get real with yourself. You have to be honest about what's keeping you from where you need to be.

Listen, I know
you want it bad,
but something's
gonna have to give, bro. You're
gonna have to drop something. You
gotta sit back and
really think
about all the
bad habits that
you do every
day that take
you further and
further away from
your goal. It's gonna be
hard to do, but it's gonna
be worth it. And you'll thank
yourself later.

It's never easy to break bad habits or exit a certain lifestyle.

In fact, it's probably one of the hardest parts of personal growth because it forces you to step outside your comfort zone. Let me tell you, being uncomfortable is something only a small percentage embrace.

But if you want something different, you have to do something different. Theo Von once said on his podcast, "Nothing changes if nothing changes."

That is a simple sentence, but it speaks volumes.

How do you expect to enter a new life when you won't let go of your old one?

In life, growth means change, and as you grow, not everyone will grow with you. That's a hard truth most people don't want to face. When you're elevating, not everyone will understand the journey you're on.

Even those you love most might start to fall behind or pull you back. It's not that they're bad people. It's just that their path isn't aligned with yours anymore.

It could be their own personal issues they throw on you, or they could be trying to drag you down because they want you to stay in the same position as they are. Some of you might have too big of a heart to let people like that go, but you have to do it if you want to grow.

In the next chapter of your life, you have to realize that not everyone is meant to walk the same path as you do.

It's not about cutting people off just to cut them off. It's about understanding that your focus, your energy, and your journey will demand sacrifices.

Some relationships might hold you back because they're tied to the version of you that you're trying to outgrow. You can't let that happen.

I had to make a lot of tough choices, leaving people behind, and it sucked. I won't lie to you. But it's necessary.

You always have to remember that some people are here for a reason and a season, and you have to know when it's time to close that chapter.

BUILD YOUR BRIDGES TO MEET YOUR GOALS

The people around you can either be your greatest asset or your biggest obstacle. If you're serious about cutting ties with the habits and mindsets that are holding you back, you need to start building bridges that connect you to your goals.

Those bridges are made of people, systems, and environments that stretch you.

Who's in your circle right now who actually sees you following through? Would they say you're reliable or just ambitious?

Those questions matter more than you think because when people trust your word, it's usually because you've built a consistent track record of action. In my life, I'm proud to say that my circle would tell you I'm reliable.

And while I hold myself to that standard, I've also learned that not everyone can or should be held to the same expectations. That's not a knock on them; it's simply recognizing that people show up in different ways, and you can't expect you from everyone.

Part of becoming a better leader is knowing people's strengths and not expecting them to be someone they're not.

But still, you need people who challenge you and sharpen you.

My brother, for example, is the one person who matches my level of reliability. We were raised the same way, so it makes sense.

I've also been shaped by my closest relationships. They've pushed me to grow as a communicator and taught me lessons that some career opportunities never could. And beyond that, I'm surrounded by people who inspire me just by how they move. Some drive me with their relentless work ethic, and others sharpen me with their strategy and perspective, correcting me when I'm off course.

That's what building bridges looks like.

Who in your life is pouring into you?

Who makes you want to rise higher, go harder, and be better?

If you can't think of anyone, that is your sign. You've got to build that bridge. Whether it's finding a mentor, a gym partner, or a business-minded friend, or even plugging into podcasts or books that challenge your mindset, do something.

Even the people you don't know personally can become sources of elevation if you're intentional about what you feed your mind.

For me, I find inspiration everywhere. I don't carry envy in my heart, so when I see others win, it motivates me.

It pushes me to assess my weaknesses and look for ways to grow.

The world becomes my teacher because I've trained myself to stay open, hungry, and humble.

If your circle doesn't push you, it's not a circle. It's a cage.

You've got to surround yourself with people who not only inspire you but also challenge you—people who won't let you slack. People who demand the best from you because they see the best in you.

And while it's important to share your goals with them, what matters more is showing them your progress.

Don't get it twisted. This Pure Journey is still yours.

You can't depend on others to walk it for you. Carry your vision.

Use their feedback and support as fuel, not dependence.

The moment you start relying on their validation to move forward is the moment you lose your identity.

So build wisely.

Build with intention.

And most of all, build with people who remind you who you said you were going to be, especially on the days you forget.

Those kinds of bridges keep you staying pure no matter what.

EMBRACE THE SACRIFICES THAT BRING RESULTS

It's a tough decision to make, but once you start cutting ties and building bridges, you'll notice a shift.

You'll start moving closer to your goals, little by little. You may not see the results immediately, and that's okay. They're coming. And when they do, you'll thank yourself for having the discipline to cut out what was blocking your blessings.

Sacrifice is part of every avenue in life—relationships, work, fitness, team success, family, and more.

Start by being brutally honest with yourself.

Identify the habits, people, and distractions that drain your time, your energy, and your potential.

Then have the courage to cut them out and replace them with what will move you forward.

It won't be easy, but if you stick with it, you'll see why it was worth it. The sooner you get started, the sooner you'll see the results you've been praying for. Ultimately, the biggest hurdle you have to jump over is yourself, so it's time to start *Cutting Ties and Building Bridges*.

Hey man, look, I need
you to understand that in this
next chapter of your life, not
everybody can come
with you. See, the
thing is, you
outgrow a lot
of people when
you're on the way
to the top. Why do
you think it's so lonely
when you get there?

PART 7

A GRATEFUL HEART

Gratitude isn't just a feeling; it's a state of being, a shift in perspective that aligns you with the essence of life itself. When you begin to truly appreciate the smallest moments, you realize that the gift isn't always in what you receive but in what you acknowledge. A heart that understands this is pure, for it knows that abundance isn't about more; it's about seeing what is with deeper eyes.

KEEP YOUR MIND STEADY

A steady mind is so necessary when you're coming up on your journey.

It's so easy to lose sight of where you are because you're always thinking about what's next.

You're focused on the outcome, and in doing so, you can miss the beauty of the process that's happening right now.

When I first started creating content in high school, I was so fixated on blowing up, getting the views, the subscribers, and the money, that I wasn't fully appreciating the opportunities to learn and grow that were right in front of me.

My mind was constantly skipping ahead to the what-ifs: *What if it doesn't work out? What if I'm not where I want to be by a certain point?*

Hey man, can you
just slow down for a
minute? I mean, just be grateful
for where you're at. I feel
like sometimes we
are so focused
on the future
that we don't
even realize
that we're in the
middle of what
we prayed for. You're
blessed. Appreciate the life
that you live because tomorrow
it can all be gone.

That kind of thinking didn't motivate me.

It made me anxious.

Eventually, I started to realize how much I was missing by always looking so far down the road.

I wasn't seeing the progress I was making, the lessons I was learning, or the ways I was already starting to change.

That's when I shifted my mentality. I started approaching every day with the concept that I had to stop expecting a harvest without planting the seeds.

You can't build a house without collecting your materials first.

You've got to be faithful to your foundation.

Each small win, each lesson, each early morning or late night is another brick laid. And when you start thinking like that—when you start showing up *today* instead of worrying about some imaginary day in the *future*—you build a foundation without even realizing it.

The key to keeping your mind grateful is understanding that joy, growth, and clarity don't come from obsessing over the future or the past. It's about appreciating the current circumstance you're in and how you can elevate from it. If you look too far ahead, you can feel anxious. If you dwell on what's behind you, you risk falling into regret. But when you center yourself in the present, fully engaged and fully aware, you discover that gratitude lives right there.

So take a pause.

Slow down.

Set your compass today.

And your future will direct itself.

DON'T TAKE YOUR LIFE FOR GRANTED

Gratitude grounds you. It slows your racing thoughts and helps you lock in on the present moment. You might not be where you want to be yet, but if you take a second and really look around, you might realize you're standing in the middle of something you once prayed for.

That's a powerful shift in perspective.

None of this is promised.

Tomorrow can change everything, and that's why you can't take today for granted.

As humans, we subconsciously fall into an entitled mentality as if we are supposed to be living the life we are chasing. I've caught myself slipping into this more than once. I used to say, *Man, I can't wait to be fully independent, handling everything myself, no help from my parents, just standing on my own.*"

Now I'm there. I take care of myself. I don't have to ask anybody for anything. And yet sometimes I forget this is exactly what I prayed for. It's a blessing, even when the pressure feels heavy. Honestly, like I said earlier, *pressure is a privilege.* It means I was given the chance to grow.

I also remember working nine-to-five jobs and thinking, *If I just had more time to create, I would really go crazy with my content.* Now I've got that time, and sometimes I still waste it.

I scroll.

I procrastinate.

I play with my hours like they're not the exact thing I used to pray for.

That's when I realize I'm taking it for granted. And I guarantee that if I had to go back to the life I used to live, I'd be mad at myself for not taking advantage of the time I've been given.

The same goes for my platforms and the impact I've been able to make.

A few years ago, I was dreaming of making videos that reached people, of being able to fund my life through a camera.

Now it's happening.

That version of me would be proud.

So how dare I let myself forget the blessing in that?

That is where entitlement starts to sneak in. And let's be clear. Entitlement and appreciation are not the same thing.

Entitlement is feeling like you're supposed to have something—like it's owed to you.

Appreciation is knowing that you didn't have to get it, but you did.

Entitlement sounds like, *Why didn't I get more?*

Appreciation says, *Wow! I got something.*

I'm not entitled to wake up every morning. I'm not owed a platform. I'm not guaranteed a single opportunity. Everything I have is from grace. God chose to wake me up today, and that alone puts me in a position of favor. When you carry that understanding, it humbles you. It makes you hold your blessings with more care and less ego.

I learned this early from my mom. As a kid, Christmases started with a mountain of gifts. But as I got older, the number of presents got smaller. At first I didn't get it. But she was teaching my brother and I. Just because we got a lot last year didn't mean we were owed the same this year.

That's a valuable lesson.

And over time, I stopped caring about the stuff. I just wanted to be with my family. That was the best gift.

Entitlement will trick you into thinking you're bigger than the program.

It makes you pout when things don't go your way.

It lowers your effort. It's that star player mentality where you think the rules don't apply to you. And when you finally get benched, you say you don't want to play anymore.

Appreciation is different.

Appreciation makes you lock in. It reminds you why you started. It makes you go harder because you know you aren't promised another chance.

So yes, aim higher. Work harder. Dream bolder. But gratitude is what keeps it pure.

Take a moment to reflect on the people around you, the opportunities you've been given, and the blessings you're sitting in right now. It doesn't mean you stop working; it means you keep working with perspective.

The real joy of success is found on the journey. It's the hardships, the constant battling, the lessons, and the struggle that shapes your character.

Appreciate the journey you've been walking because it's the best part of the whole experience. You're becoming the person you once hoped you could be.

Don't take it for granted.

Live with appreciation.

Let it keep you grounded.

Let it keep you pure.

ACKNOWLEDGE YOUR BLESSINGS

It may be hard to see your purpose clearly right now, especially if you're not where you want to be. But here's one of the biggest signs that you're meant to do something with your life: God chose to wake you up today. Out of all the billions of people on earth and the many people who died, you were picked to continue and contribute to the world.

Gratitude isn't just about saying thank you. It's about how you carry yourself, how you approach the day. When I started practicing just being thankful for waking up, for completing the day, and for the small blessings, it made me a more grounded person.

It helped me live with more freedom and focus because when you live like tomorrow's not promised, you start to really value today.

People don't really value life. I wake up, and it's a blessing to be alive. Every time I pray, I thank God for another day of life, thank you God for another chance to get it right. You know how many people already died today? The fact I woke up is favor.

That doesn't mean you become complacent either.

I'm grateful for everything I have. And I still want more.

That's not a contradiction. It's a mindset. You can have hunger and humility at the same time. You can work for the future without becoming blind to the beauty of the present.

Here's the truth: If you don't appreciate your situation, why would God open up more doors? Why would He give you more to carry if you're not even grateful for what's currently in your hands?

We don't even deserve God's love or grace, yet He gives them as gifts—not because we're entitled but because He is good. Understand that truth. Then having a heart of gratitude can take you to heights you never imagined. Sometimes God just wants you to appreciate the gift of life He is giving you before you can start really living.

That's why I try to recognize the little things—walking outside on my own two legs, adjusting the thermostat, turning on clean water without thinking twice. You might be reading this book in a house with running water, lights on, food in the fridge, and shoes on your feet. Those are blessings. And someone somewhere is praying for the life you already have.

Valuing life helps you focus on what truly matters and align with your inner values. Even if your path isn't clear, it's still a privilege and blessing that you get to walk it.

All this starts by being present in your life.

To live more fully in the now, start by slowing down and truly thinking about the abilities and resources you have that you overlook.

Practice gratitude daily, even for the smallest joys around you. This simple habit can transform your perspective. Focus on one task at a time and reduce distractions like screen time to truly connect with your surroundings. Set an intention each morning to be present, and allow yourself brief pauses throughout the day to reset and recenter.

Celebrate your small victories as they come. Let each one remind you of the richness in everyday moments. By choosing to approach life that way, you can transform your daily routine into a series of intentional, deeply meaningful experiences that will help you feel more grounded, grateful, and connected to the beauty of the present.

START JOURNALING

An exercise that has always helped me is journaling. I encourage everyone to journal every day. When you journal, it's almost as if you're creating a record of your current state of mind and the place you're at in life, capturing moments of growth, challenges you've overcome, and insights you've gained over time.

That can be especially helpful during tough periods since looking back on past entries can remind you of your resilience and progress. Writing daily or even weekly entries builds a habit of self-awareness that encourages intentional living and fosters gratitude.

In times of stress, journaling can serve as a healthy outlet to release stress and sort through overwhelming emotions. It becomes a safe, private space where you can explore thoughts honestly without judgment.

Whether you're reflecting on your day, setting goals, or expressing gratitude, journaling encourages you to live with greater awareness and helps you stay connected to your purpose and stay grounded. Incorporating journaling into your life can be as simple as starting with a few minutes a day, creating a routine of reflection that strengthens self-understanding, deepens gratitude, and ultimately supports mental and emotional well-being.

WHATEVER YOU DO, STAY PURE

Listen, I want you to value the life you live.

You are here for a reason, and life has so much to offer you. Don't worry about what happened yesterday; you will never get that day back. Value today and be present in the moment so you can enjoy your tomorrow.

Your journey isn't just about the destination; it's about the *transformation* that occurs along the way.

Life will present countless challenges, opportunities, and moments of reflection, but the true essence of this journey lies in the person you become through it all.

Every step you take is carving out a path to the truest version of yourself. And once you discover who that person truly is, the journey shifts from one of seeking to one of becoming. In that pursuit, staying true to yourself is the ultimate act of staying pure. But the dangerous part is if you lose sight of that, you can lose yourself completely.

You can get so wrapped up in chasing status, approval, and success that you slowly drift away from who you really are. And the scariest part is that you won't even notice it's happening until one day you look in the mirror and don't recognize the person staring back at you. You've built an image that looks impressive on the outside but feels dead on the inside. You've created a version of yourself you can't even stand to live with.

Most people don't talk about this part of the journey—the dark side that creeps in without warning. It lures you with pride, control, and the illusion of importance. It convinces you that more is always better, even if it costs you your peace, your relationships, and your soul. That kind of "success" doesn't just cost a lot; it costs everything. And it will never be worth the price.

That's why I never want to lose myself.

No matter how high I climb, I want to remain grounded, centered, and aligned with who I truly am.

Real success isn't just about external wins; it's about spiritual growth.

It's about being rich in values—about walking in peace, purpose, and clarity.

If you're chasing things that require you to betray who you are, it's not pure.

No amount of fame, status, or money is worth losing your soul.

True purity is found in that tension—being ambitious while staying content, remaining hungry while still grateful, and striving for more without abandoning your integrity.

So don't get it twisted. Go after your dreams. Work hard. Push yourself. But as you rise, protect your soul because that's the part of you the world can't take away. And it's the part of you that makes everything else meaningful.

The beauty of this journey is that it is yours alone. It is in the quiet moments of self-reflection, struggles, and victories that you will uncover the power to be unapologetically you. The essence of Purity is learning to live in your truest form and not the version the world pressures you to be. It's about loosening the grip of expectation and performance, and finding the freedom to just be yourself. And when you live from that place, even your work, your passion, and your presence carry authenticity. At the end of the day, the greatest gift you can give the world is yourself, and nobody else can offer that but you.

As you continue your journey, remember that the truest form of success is not found in external achievements but in the peace and fulfillment that come with staying true to who you are.

Your purest self is waiting to blossom. Trust in the teachings this journey will give you because you were meant to learn them. A lot of people get caught up in being someone they aren't, and they end up on a journey that was never meant to be theirs. By staying true to who you are and trusting the process, you will discover your deepest purpose and experience a freedom unlike any other.

This is the spirit of what it means to stay pure. You'll be grateful when you realize that no matter what room you enter, you're yourself no matter what. And in the end, you will realize that this is, without a doubt, *a Pure Journey.*

ACKNOWLEDGMENTS

I'd like to thank:

Pastor J. C. Worley, an early mentor whose example gave me someone to look up to.

Coach Harris, my youth coach, who first pushed me to dig deep and discover my grit.

Ron Edwards, my high school teacher whose kindness and positivity left a lasting impression.

Coach Dre, my basketball coach who became the steady voice I needed during one of the hardest seasons of my life.

To my close friends, thank you for standing with me through this journey.

ABOUT THE AUTHOR

Damii (Dami Onakoya) is a content creator, entrepreneur, and cultural voice whose work bridges entertainment, lifestyle, and motivation. Best known for his YouTube channels *Damii* and *DamiiBTS*, he has built a global community drawn to his authenticity, humor, and ability to spark both laughter and reflection through his work.

At the heart of Damii's creative journey is his signature philosophy, **Stay Pure**—a message that encourages authenticity, comfort in one's own skin, and resilience in a world full of distractions. What began as a personal mantra fueled the creation of **Onacero**, his lifestyle brand, and has since grown into a movement that inspires people to live with intention and stay true to themselves.

Damii's path is one of constant reinvention, driven by a relentless pursuit of elevation, humor, and impact. His work defies categories—blending storytelling, culture, and lifestyle into a vision that is as inspiring as it is original. With his debut book, he breaks new ground as a modern creator stepping into literature, proving that his voice reaches far beyond the screen. More than just a content creator, Damii is bridging culture, identity, and purpose—pushing forward a movement bigger than himself. What he creates today is only the beginning of a legacy that will echo far beyond him.

www.ingramcontent.com/pod-product-compliance
Lightning Source LLC
Chambersburg PA
CBHW070925130626
46555CB00001B/293